Fresh

from the

Hearth

Fresh from the Hearth

100 Healthy, Heartwarming Recipes for Quick Breads, Muffins, and Coffeecakes

A HEALTHY EXCHANGES® COOKBOOK

JoAnna M. Lund

HELPing Others HELP Themselves
the **Healthy Exchanges®** Way™

A Perigee Book

This cookbook is dedicated to the entire QVC "family," from the viewers who love my easy "common folk" healthy recipes, to the book buyers who are always interested in my newest projects, to the show hosts who are so delightful to work with, to the production staff who work so hard to ensure everything goes as planned without a glitch, and to the hardworking order representatives answering the phones. Each of you is a vital part of our recipe for success.

A Perigee Book
Published by The Berkley Publishing Group
A member of Penguin Putnam Inc.
375 Hudson Street
New York, New York 10014

Copyright © 1999 by Healthy Exchanges, Inc.
Diabetic Exchanges calculated by Rose Hoenig, R.D., L.D.
Cover design by Charles Björklund
Cover art by Charles Björklund and Joe Krantz
Front-cover author photograph by Glamour Shots® of West Des Moines

For more information about Healthy Exchanges products, contact:
Healthy Exchanges, Inc.
P.O. Box 124
DeWitt, Iowa 52742-0124
(319) 659-8234

Perigee Special Sales edition: January 1999
ISBN: 0-399-52527-0
Published simultaneously in Canada.

The Penguin Putnam Inc. World Wide Web site address is
http://www.penguinputnam.com

Printed in the United States of America

10 9 8 7 6 5 4 3 2 1

Before using the recipes and advice in this book, consult your physician or health-care provider to be sure they are appropriate for you. The information in this book is not intended to take the place of any medical advice. It reflects the author's experiences, studies, research, and opinions regarding a healthy lifestyle. All material included in this publication is believed to be accurate. The publisher assumes no responsibility for any health, welfare, or subsequent damage that might be incurred from the use of these materials.

Contents

Acknowledgments

I'm so thankful to all the wonderful people at QVC who help me share my "common folk" healthy recipe books with you— throughout the year *and* on those oh-so-special days that I get to offer you my Today's Special Value trio of books. For helping me get my collection of cookbooks ready for that glorious moment the floor producer says, "You're on," I want to thank:

Paula Piercy and Karen Foner from QVC, for giving my books the honor of being a TSV, and John Duff and Barbara O'Shea from Putnam, for helping me get those books published quickly so they are ready for the big day.

Angela Miller and Coleen O'Shea, for believing in this middle-aged grandma from Iowa who writes in a "Grandma Moses" style.

Rita Ahlers, Connie Schultz, Shirley Morrow, Lori Hansen, and all my other Healthy Exchanges employees who help me get my manuscripts out the door in a timely fashion.

Barbara Alpert and Rose Hoenig, R.D., L.D., for helping with the more technical sides of what I do. Barbara makes sure I use the right words so you can understand what I write and Rose double-checks my ingredients so that anyone concerned with health can use my recipes with complete confidence.

Cliff Lund and everyone in my family, who support my mission of "common folk" healthy recipes and a commonsense approach to healthy living.

God, for giving me the talent to do what I do and for ensuring that both Putnam and QVC would come into my life at the right moment.

Why Baking Is Better When You Do It with Love

Is there anything more cozy and comforting than blueberry muffins served piping hot in a pretty napkin-draped basket? Or perhaps a fragrant slice of nut-studded banana bread, or a piece of luscious homemade coffeecake?

Why, my mouth just starts watering at the thought of how that first fresh-baked bite will taste!

Yours, too? I'm not surprised! Ever since fire was first discovered, people from all over the world and from every culture have been enjoying the special culinary magic of baked goods. Our dearest memories of gathering at Grandma's table on family occasions always seem to include some bread or cake prepared especially for us in her great big oven. And the recipes for these unforgettably good treats have been handed down from generation to generation, as far back as anyone can remember.

Trouble is, of course, that what made those cakes and breads and muffins so irresistibly tasty was usually the sugar and the shortening! So when you became concerned about losing weight or managing your cholesterol, coping with diabetes or recovering from a heart attack, those recipes were among the first to be relegated to the back of the recipe box. You missed them with all your heart, but you figured you had no choice.

The good news is, you *do* have a choice. Here's a delicious collection of baked goods of all kinds, jam-packed with delectable ingredients and flavor—but low in fat and low in sugar. Now you can enjoy the foods you love without fear or guilt, and without settling for a bland and tasteless "diet" version of your favorites.

Let me share some of my best healthy ideas for baking up a storm!

- No time to bake because you need to spend time with your kids? Bring them along to the kitchen and put them to work—spraying muffin tins, stirring up dry ingredients, keeping an eye through the little oven window on how your bread is doing. It will make them feel important and, better yet, closer to you.

- Make your baked goods turn out better by starting out right: toss your old bag of flour and buy a new one; store your nonfat milk powder in the refrigerator to keep it longer; open a fresh box of baking soda; treat yourself to a new non-stick pan instead of using an old one covered with scratches; start a strawberry patch now so you can enjoy fresh berries in your recipes come summer.

- Transform baking from a chore into a special hobby by becoming the baker you always hoped to be. Try out lots of recipes until you find the ones you like best, then make those your signature contribution to charity bake sales or a child's classroom party. Give a recipe box filled with hand-written healthy recipe cards to your niece for her wedding shower gift.

- Remember that baking is a complex combination of actions and possibilities. If your bread or muffins turn out a little dry, don't take it personally—just try again and shorten the baking time! If your coffeecake tastes a bit "rubbery," don't be quite so energetic when you mix up the dough; save that intensity for creating a pretty centerpiece for the breakfast table! If you live at a high altitude or in a very dry climate, your baked goods will turn out differently than if you live at sea level or in a very humid spot. I usually recommend checking for doneness about 5 to 10 minutes before my listed baking time. (For example, if I tell you to bake a quick bread for one hour, the first time you prepare it I recommend checking if it's baked through after about 45 or 50 minutes. You'll be glad you did!)

- Share what you love, and start new traditions that other family members will cherish. If you've never had a holiday goodie exchange, why not organize one next year for your closest friends or colleagues at the office? Make a habit of giving fresh-baked gifts to the people you love, and feel proud that you're also sharing the gift of good health!

Dear Friends,

People often ask me why I include the same general information at the beginning of all my cookbooks. If you've seen any of my other books, you'll know that my "common folk" recipes are just one part of the Healthy Exchanges picture. You know that I firmly believe—and say so whenever and wherever I can—that *Healthy Exchanges is not a diet, it's a way of life!* That's why I include the story of Healthy Exchanges in every book, because I know that the tale of my struggle to lose weight and regain my health is one that speaks to the hearts of many thousands of people. And because Healthy Exchanges is not just a collection of recipes, I always include the wisdom that I've learned from my own experiences and the knowledge of the health and cooking professionals I meet. Whether it's learning about nutrition or making shopping and cooking easier, no Healthy Exchanges book would be complete without features like "A Peek into My Pantry" or "JoAnna's Ten Commandments of Successful Cooking."

Even if you've read my other books, you might still want to skim the following chapters—you never know when I'll slip in a new bit of wisdom or suggest a new product that will make your journey to health an easier and tastier one. If you're sharing this book with a friend or family member, you'll want to make sure they read the following pages before they start stirring up the recipes.

If this is the first book of mine that you've read, I want to welcome you with all my heart to the Healthy Exchanges Family. (And, of course, I'd love to hear your comments or questions. See the back of the book for my mailing address . . . or come visit if you happen to find yourself in DeWitt, Iowa—just ask anybody for directions to Healthy Exchanges!)

Jo Anna

JoAnna M. Lund
and Healthy
Exchanges

Food is the first invited guest to every special occasion in every family's memory scrapbook. From baptism to graduation, from weddings to wakes, food brings us together.

It wasn't always that way at our house. I used to eat alone, even when my family was there, because while they were dining on real food, I was nibbling at whatever my newest diet called for. In fact, for twenty-eight years, I called myself the diet queen of DeWitt, Iowa.

I tried every diet I ever came across, every one I could afford, and every one that found its way to my small town in eastern Iowa. I was willing to try anything that promised to "melt off the pounds," determined to deprive my body in every possible way in order to become thin at last.

I sent away for expensive "miracle" diet pills. I starved myself on the Cambridge Diet and the Bahama Diet. I gobbled diet candies, took thyroid pills, fiber pills, prescription and over-the-counter diet pills. I went to endless weight-loss support group meetings—but I somehow managed to turn healthy programs such as Overeaters Anonymous, Weight Watchers, and TOPS into unhealthy diets . . . diets I could never follow for more than a few months.

I was determined to discover something that worked long-term, but each new failure increased my desperation that I'd never find it.

I ate strange concoctions and rubbed on even stranger potions. I tried liquid diets. I agreed to be hypnotized. I tried reflexology and even had an acupressure device stuck in my ear!

Does my story sound a lot like yours? I'm not surprised. No wonder the weight-loss business is a billion-dollar industry!

Every new thing I tried seemed to work—at least at first. And losing that first five or ten pounds would get me so excited, I'd believe that this new miracle diet would, finally, get my weight off for keeps.

Inevitably, though, the initial excitement wore off. The diet's routine and boredom set in, and I quit. I shoved the pills to the back of the medicine chest; pushed the cans of powdered shake mix to the rear of the kitchen cabinets; slid all the program materials out of sight under my bed; and once more I felt like a failure.

Like most dieters, I quickly gained back the weight I'd lost each time, along with a few extra "souvenir" pounds that seemed always to settle around my hips. I'd done the diet-lose-weight-gain-it-all-back "yo-yo" on the average of once a year. It's no exaggeration to say that over the years I've lost 1,000 pounds—and gained back 1,150 pounds.

Finally, at the age of forty-six, I weighed more than I'd ever imagined possible. I'd stopped believing that any diet could work for me. I drowned my sorrows in sacks of cake doughnuts and wondered if I'd live long enough to watch my grandchildren grow up.

Something had to change.

I had to change.

Finally, I did.

I'm just over fifty now—and I'm 130 pounds less than my all-time high of close to 300 pounds. I've kept the weight off for more than six years. I'd like to lose another ten pounds, but I'm not obsessed about it. If it takes me two or three years to accomplish it, that's okay.

What I *do* care about is never saying hello again to any of those unwanted pounds I said good-bye to!

How did I jump off the roller coaster I was on? For one thing, I finally stopped looking to food to solve my emotional problems. But what really shook me up—and got me started on the path that changed my life—was Operation Desert Storm in early 1991. I sent three children off to the Persian Gulf War—my son-in-law, Matt, a medic in Special Forces; my daughter, Becky, a full-time college student and member of a medical unit in the Army Reserve; and my son, James, a member of the Inactive Army Reserve, reactivated as a chemicals expert.

Somehow, knowing that my children were putting their lives on the line got me thinking about my own mortality—and I knew in my heart the last thing they needed while they were overseas was to get a letter from home saying that their mother was ill because of a food-related problem.

The day I drove the third child to the airport to leave for Saudi Arabia, something happened to me that would change my life for the better—and forever. I stopped praying my constant prayer as a professional dieter, which was simply "Please, God, let me lose ten pounds by Friday." Instead, I began praying, "God, please help me not to be a burden to my kids and my family." I quit praying for what I wanted and started praying for what I needed—and in the process my prayers were answered. I couldn't keep the kids safe— that was out of my hands—but I could try to get healthier to better handle the stress of it. It was the least I could do on the homefront.

That quiet prayer was the beginning of the new JoAnna Lund. My initial goal was not to lose weight or create healthy recipes. I only wanted to become healthier for my kids, my husband, and myself.

Each of my children returned safely from the Persian Gulf War. But something didn't come back—the 130 extra pounds I'd been lugging around for far too long. I'd finally accepted the truth after all those agonizing years of suffering through on-again, off-again dieting.

There are no "magic" cures in life.

No "miracle" potion, pill, or diet will make unwanted pounds disappear.

I found something better than magic, if you can believe it. When I turned my weight and health dilemma over to God for guidance, a new JoAnna Lund and Healthy Exchanges were born.

I discovered a new way to live my life—and uncovered an unexpected talent for creating easy "common folk" healthy recipes and sharing my commonsense approach to healthy living. I learned that I could motivate others to change their lives and adopt a positive outlook. I began publishing cookbooks and a monthly food newsletter, and speaking to groups all over the country.

I like to say, "*When life handed me a lemon, not only did I make healthy, tasty lemonade, I wrote the recipe down!*"

What I finally found was not a quick fix or a short-term diet, but a great way to live well for a lifetime.

I want to share it with you.

Food Exchanges and Weight Loss Choices™

If you've ever been on one of the national weight-loss programs like Weight Watchers or Diet Center, you've already been introduced to the concept of measured portions of different food groups that make up your daily food plan. If you are not familiar with such a system of weight-loss choices or exchanges, here's a brief explanation. (If you want or need more detailed information, you can write to the American Dietetic Association or the American Diabetes Association for comprehensive explanations.)

The idea of food exchanges is to divide foods into basic food groups. The foods in each group are measured in servings that have comparable values. These groups include Proteins/Meats, Breads/Starches, Fruits, Skim Milk, Vegetables, Fats, Free Foods, and Optional Calories.

Each choice or exchange included in a particular group has about the same number of calories and a similar carbohydrate, protein, and fat content as the other foods in that group. Because any food on a particular list can be "exchanged" for any other food in that group, it makes sense to call the food groups *exchanges* or *choices*.

I like to think we are also "exchanging" bad habits and food choices for good ones!

By using Weight Loss Choices or exchanges, you can choose from a variety of foods without having to calculate the nutrient value of each one. This makes it easier to include a wide variety of foods in your daily menus and gives you the opportunity to tailor your choices to your unique appetite.

If you want to lose weight, you should consult your physician or other weight-control expert regarding the number of servings that would be best for you from each food group. Since men generally require more calories than women, and since the requirements for growing children and teenagers differ from those of adults, the right number of exchange for any one person is a personal decision.

I have included a suggested plan of Weight Loss Choices in the pages following the exchange lists. It's a program I used to lose 130 pounds, and it's the one I still follow today.

(If you are a diabetic or have been diagnosed with heart problems, it is best to meet with your physician before using this or any other food program or recipe collection.)

Food Group Weight Loss Choices™/Exchanges

Not all food group exchanges are alike. The ones that follow are for anyone who's interested in weight loss or maintenance. If you are a diabetic, you should check with your health-care provider or dietitian to get the information you need to help you plan your diet. Diabetic exchanges are calculated by the American Diabetic Association, and information about them is provided in *The Diabetic's Healthy Exchanges Cookbook* (Perigee Books).

Every Healthy Exchanges recipe provides calculations in three ways:

- Weight Loss Choices/Exchanges

- Calories; Fat, Protein, Carbohydrates, and Fiber grams; and Sodium and Calcium milligrams

- Diabetic Exchanges calculated for me by a registered dietitian

Healthy Exchanges recipes can help you eat well and recover your health, whatever your health concerns may be. Please take a few minutes to review the exchange lists and the suggestions that follow on how to count them. You have lots of great eating in store for you!

Proteins

Meat, poultry, seafood, eggs, cheese, and legumes. One exchange of Protein is approximately 60 calories. Examples of one Protein choice or exchange:

1 ounce cooked weight of lean meat, poultry, or seafood
2 ounces white fish
1½ ounces 97% fat-free ham
1 egg (limit to no more than 4 per week)
¼ cup egg substitute
3 egg whites
¾ ounce reduced-fat cheese
½ cup fat-free cottage cheese
2 ounces cooked or ¾ ounce uncooked dry beans
1 tablespoon peanut butter (also count 1 fat exchange)

Breads

Breads, crackers, cereals, grains, and starchy vegetables. One exchange of Bread is approximately 80 calories. Examples of one Bread choice or exchange:

1 slice bread or 2 slices reduced-calorie bread (40 calories or less)
1 roll, any type (1 ounce)
½ cup cooked pasta or ¾ ounce uncooked (scant ½ cup)
½ cup cooked rice or 1 ounce uncooked (⅓ cup)
3 tablespoons flour
¾ ounce cold cereal
½ cup cooked hot cereal or ¾ ounce uncooked (2 tablespoons)
½ cup corn (kernels or cream-style) or peas
4 ounces white potato, cooked, or 5 ounces uncooked

3 ounces sweet potato, cooked, or 4 ounces uncooked
3 cups air-popped popcorn
7 fat-free crackers (¾ ounce)
3 (2½-inch squares) graham crackers
2 (¾-ounce) rice cakes or 6 mini
1 tortilla, any type (6-inch diameter)

Fruits

All fruits and fruit juices. One exchange of Fruit is approximately 60 calories. Examples of one Fruit choice or exchange:

1 small apple or ½ cup slices
1 small orange
½ medium banana
¾ cup berries (except strawberries and cranberries)
1 cup strawberries or cranberries
½ cup canned fruit, packed in fruit juice or rinsed well
2 tablespoons raisins
1 tablespoon spreadable fruit spread
½ cup apple juice (4 fluid ounces)
½ cup orange juice (4 fluid ounces)
½ cup applesauce

Skim Milk

Milk, buttermilk, and yogurt. One exchange of Skim Milk is approximately 90 calories. Examples of one Skim Milk choice or exchange:

1 cup skim milk
½ cup evaporated skim milk
1 cup low-fat buttermilk
¾ cup plain fat-free yogurt
⅓ cup nonfat dry milk powder

Vegetables

All fresh, canned, or frozen vegetables other than the starchy vegetables. One exchange of Vegetable is approximately 30 calories. Examples of one Vegetable choice or exchange:

½ cup vegetable
¼ cup tomato sauce
1 medium fresh tomato
½ cup vegetable juice

Fats

Margarine, mayonnaise, vegetable oils, salad dressings, olives, and nuts. One exchange of Fat is approximately 40 calories. Examples of one Fat choice or exchange:

1 teaspoon margarine or 2 teaspoons reduced-calorie margarine
1 teaspoon butter
1 teaspoon vegetable oil
1 teaspoon mayonnaise or 2 teaspoons reduced-calorie mayonnaise
1 teaspoon peanut butter
1 ounce olives
¼ ounce pecans or walnuts

Free Foods

Foods that do not provide nutritional value but are used to enhance the taste of foods are included in the Free Foods group. Examples of these are spices, herbs, extracts, vinegar, lemon juice, mustard, Worcestershire sauce, and soy sauce. Cooking sprays and artificial sweeteners used in moderation are also included in this group. However, you'll see that I include the caloric value of artificial sweeteners in the Optional Calories of the recipes.

You may occasionally see a recipe that lists "free food" as part of the portion. According to the published exchange lists, a free food contains fewer than 20 calories per serving. Two or three servings per day of free foods/drinks are usually allowed in a meal plan.

Optional Calories

Foods that do not fit into any other group but are used in moderation in recipes are included in Optional Calories. Foods that are counted in this way include sugar-free gelatin and puddings, fat-free mayonnaise and dressings, reduced-calorie whipped toppings, reduced-calorie syrups and jams, chocolate chips, coconut, and canned broth.

Sliders™

These are 80 Optional Calorie increments that do not fit into any particular category. You can choose which food group to *slide* these into. It is wise to limit this selection to approximately three to four per day to ensure the best possible nutrition for your body while still enjoying an occasional treat.

Sliders may be used in either of the following ways:

1. If you have consumed all your Protein, Bread, Fruit, or Skim Milk Weight Loss Choices for the day and you want to eat additional foods from those food groups, you simply use a Slider. It's what I call "healthy horse trading." Remember that Sliders may not be traded for choices in the Vegetables or Fats food groups.

2. Sliders may also be deducted from your Optional Calories for the day or week. ¼ Slider equals 20 Optional Calories; ½ Slider equals 40 Optional Calories; ¾ Slider equals 60 Optional Calories; and 1 Slider equals 80 Optional Calories.

Healthy Exchanges® Weight Loss Choices™

My original Healthy Exchanges program of Weight Loss Choices was based on an average daily total of 1,400 to 1,600 calories per day. That was what I determined was right for my needs, and for those of most women. Because men require additional calories (about 1,600 to 1,900), here are my suggested plans for women and men. (*If you require more or fewer calories, please revise this plan to meet your individual needs.*)

Each day, women should plan to eat:

2 Skim Milk servings, 90 calories each
2 Fat servings, 40 calories each
3 Fruit servings, 60 calories each
4 Vegetable servings, or more, 30 calories each
5 Protein servings, 60 calories each
5 Bread servings, 80 calories each

Each day, men should plan to eat:

2 Skim Milk servings, 90 calories each
4 Fat servings, 40 calories each
3 Fruit servings, 60 calories each
4 Vegetable servings, or more, 30 calories each
6 Protein servings, 60 calories each
7 Bread servings, 80 calories each

Young people should follow the program for men but add 1 Skim Milk serving for a total of 3 servings.

You may also choose to add up to 100 Optional Calories per day, and up to 21 to 28 Sliders per week at 80 calories each. If you choose to include more Sliders in your daily or weekly totals, deduct those 80 calories from your Optional Calorie "bank."

A word about **Sliders**: These are to be counted toward your totals after you have used your allotment of choices of Skim Milk, Protein, Bread, and Fruit for the day. By "sliding" an additional choice into one of these groups, you can meet your individual needs for that day. Sliders are especially helpful when traveling, stressed-out, eating out, or for special events. I often use mine so I can enjoy my favorite Healthy Exchanges desserts. Vegetables are not to be counted as Sliders. Enjoy as many Vegetable choices as you need to feel satisfied. Because we want to limit our fat intake to moderate amounts, additional Fat choices should not be counted as Sliders. If you choose to include more fat on an *occasional* basis, count the extra choices as Optional Calories.

Keep a daily food diary of your Weight Loss Choices, checking off what you eat as you go. If, at the end of the day, your required selections are not 100 percent accounted for, but you have done the best you can, go to bed with a clear conscience. There will be days when you have ¼ Fruit or ½ Bread left over. What are you going to do—eat two slices of an orange or half a slice of bread and throw the rest out? I always say, "Nothing in life comes out exact." Just do the best you can . . . *the best you can.*

Try to drink at least eight 8-ounce glasses of water a day. Water truly is the "nectar" of good health.

As a little added insurance, I take a multivitamin each day. It's not essential, but if my day's worth of well-planned meals "bites the dust" when unexpected events intrude on my regular routine, my body still gets its vital nutrients.

The calories listed in each group of choices are averages. Some choices within each group may be higher or lower, so it's important to select a variety of different foods instead of eating the same three or four all the time.

Use your Optional Calories! They are what I call "life's little extras." They make all the difference in how you enjoy your food and appreciate the variety available to you. Yes, we can get by without them, but do you really want to? Keep in mind that you should be using all your daily Weight Loss Choices first to ensure you are getting the basics of good nutrition. But I guarantee that Optional Calories will keep you from feeling deprived—and help you reach your weight-loss goals.

Sodium, Fat, Cholesterol, and Processed Foods

A re Healthy Exchanges ingredients really healthy?
When I first created Healthy Exchanges, many people asked about sodium; about whether it was necessary to calculate the percentage of fat, saturated fat, and cholesterol in a healthy diet; and about my use of processed foods in many recipes. I researched these questions as I was developing my program, so you can feel confident about using the recipes and food plan.

Sodium

Most people consume more sodium than their bodies need. The American Heart Association and the American Diabetes Association recommend limiting daily sodium intake to no more than 3,000 milligrams per day. If your doctor suggests you limit your sodium even more, then *you really must read labels.*

Sodium is an essential nutrient and should not be completely eliminated. It helps to regulate blood volume and is needed for normal daily muscle and nerve functions. Most of us, however, have no trouble getting "all we need" and then some.

As with everything else, moderation is my approach. I rarely ever have salt on my list as an added ingredient. But if you're especially sodium-sensitive, make the right choices for you—and save high-sodium foods such as sauerkraut for an occasional treat.

I use lots of spices to enhance flavors, so you won't notice the absence of salt. In the few cases where it is used, salt is vital for the success of the recipe, so please don't omit it.

When I do use an ingredient high in sodium, I try to compensate by using low-sodium products in the remainder of the recipe. Many fat-free products are a little higher in sodium to make up for any loss of flavor that disappeared along with the fat. But when I take advantage of these fat-free, higher-sodium products, I stretch that ingredient within the recipe, lowering the amount of sodium per serving. A good example is my use of fat-free and reduced-sodium canned soups. While the suggested number of servings per can is two, I make sure my final creation serves at least four and sometimes six. So the soup's sodium has been "watered down" from one-third to one-half of the original amount.

Even if you don't have to watch your sodium intake for medical reasons, using moderation is another "healthy exchange" to make on your own journey to good health.

Fat Percentages

We've been told that 30 percent is the magic number—that we should limit fat intake to 30 percent or less of our total calories. It's good advice, and I try to have a weekly average of 15 percent to 25 percent myself. I believe any less than 15 percent is really just another restrictive diet that won't last. And more than 25 percent on a regular basis is too much of a good thing.

When I started listing fat grams along with calories in my recipes, I was tempted to include the percentage of calories from fat. After all, in the vast majority of my recipes, that percentage is well below 30 percent. This even includes my pie recipes that allow you a realistic serving instead of many "diet" recipes that tell you a serving is $1/12$ of a pie.

Figuring fat grams is easy enough. Each gram of fat equals 9 calories. Multiply fat grams by 9, then divide that number by the total calories to get the percentage of calories from fat.

So why don't I do it? After consulting four registered dietitians for advice, I decided to omit this information. They felt that it's too easy for people to become obsessed by that 30 percent figure, which is after all supposed to be a percentage of total calories over the course of a day or a week. We mustn't feel we can't include a healthy ingredient such as pecans or olives in one recipe just because, on its own, it has more than 30 percent of its calories from fat.

An example of this would be a casserole made with 90 percent lean red meat. Most of us benefit from eating red meat in moderation, as it provides iron and niacin in our diets, and it also makes life more enjoyable for us and those who eat with us. If we *only* look at the percentage of calories from fat in a serving of this one dish, which might be as high as 40 to 45 percent, we might choose not to include this recipe in our weekly food plan.

The dietitians suggested that it's important to consider the total picture when making such decisions. As long as your overall food plan keeps fat calories to 30 percent, it's all right to enjoy an occasional dish that is somewhat higher in fat content. Healthy foods I include in **MODERATION** include 90 percent lean red meat, olives, and nuts. I don't eat these foods every day, and you may not either. But occasionally, in a good recipe, they make all the difference in the world between just getting by (deprivation) and truly enjoying your food.

Remember, the goal is eating in a healthy way so you can enjoy and live well the rest of your life.

Saturated Fats and Cholesterol

You'll see that I don't provide calculations for saturated fats or cholesterol amounts in my recipes. It's for the simple and yet not so simple reason that accurate, up-to-date, brand-specific information can be difficult to obtain from food manufacturers, especially since the way in which they produce food keeps changing rapidly. But once more I've consulted with registered dietitians and other professionals and found that, because I use only a few products that are high in saturated fat, and use them in such limited quantities, my recipes are suitable for patients concerned about controlling or lowering cholesterol. You'll also find that whenever I do use one of these ingredients *in moderation*, everything else in the recipe, and in the meals my family and I enjoy, is low in fat.

Processed Foods

Just what is processed food, anyway? What do I mean by the term "processed foods," and why do I use them, when the "purest" recipe developers in Recipe Land consider them "pedestrian" and won't ever use something from a box, container, or can? A letter I received and a passing statement from a stranger made me reflect on what I mean when I refer to processed foods, and helped me reaffirm why I use them in my "common folk" healthy recipes.

If you are like the vast millions who agree with me, then I'm not sharing anything new with you. And if you happen to disagree, that's okay, too. After all, this is America, the Land of the Free. We are blessed to live in a great nation where we can all believe what we want about anything.

A few months ago, a woman sent me several articles from various "whole food" publications and wrote that she was wary of processed foods, and wondered why I used them in my recipes. She then scribbled on the bottom of her note, "Just how healthy is Healthy Exchanges?" Then, a few weeks later, during a chance visit at a public food event with a very pleasant woman, I was struck by how we all have our own definitions of what processed foods are. She shared with me, in a somewhat self-righteous manner, that she never uses processed foods. She only cooked with fresh fruits and vegetables, she told me. Then later she said that she used canned reduced-fat soups all the time! Was her definition different than mine, I wondered? Soup in a can, whether it's reduced in fat or not, still meets my definition of a processed food.

So I got out a copy of my book *HELP: Healthy Exchanges Lifetime Plan* and reread what I had written back then about processed foods. Nothing in my definition had changed since I wrote that section. I still believe that healthy processed foods, such as canned soups, prepared piecrusts, sugar-free instant puddings, fat-free sour cream, and frozen whipped topping, when used properly, all have a place as ingredients in healthy recipes.

I never use an ingredient that hasn't been approved by either the American Diabetic Association, the American Dietetic Association, or the American Heart Association. Whenever I'm in doubt, I send for their position papers, then ask knowledgeable registered dietitians to explain those papers to me in layman's language. I've been assured by all of them that the sugar- and fat-free products I use in my recipes are indeed safe.

If you don't agree, nothing I can say or write will convince you otherwise. But, if you've been using the healthy processed foods and have been concerned about the almost daily hoopla you hear about yet another product that's going to be the doom of all of us, then just stick with reason. For every product on the grocery shelves, there are those who want you to buy it and there are those who don't, *because they want you to buy their products instead.* So we have to learn to sift the fact from the fiction. Let's take sugar substitutes, for example. In making your own evaluations, you should be skeptical about any information provided by the sugar substitute manufacturers, because they have a vested interest in our buying their products. Likewise, ignore any information provided by the sugar industry, because they have a vested interest in our *not* buying sugar substitutes. Then, if you aren't sure if you can really trust the government or any of its agencies, toss out their data, too. That leaves the three associations I mentioned earlier. Do you think any of them would say a product is safe if it isn't? Or say a product isn't safe when it is? They have nothing to gain or lose, *other than their integrity*, if they intentionally try to mislead us. That's why I only go to these associations for information concerning healthy processed foods.

I certainly don't recommend that everything we eat should come from a can, box, or jar. I think the best of all possible worlds is to start with the basics: grains such as rice, pasta, or corn. Then, for example, add some raw vegetables and extra-lean meat such as poultry, fish, beef, or pork. Stir in some healthy canned soup or tomato sauce, and you'll end up with something that is not only healthy but tastes so good, everyone from toddlers to great-grandparents will want to eat it!

I've never been in favor of spraying everything we eat with chemicals, and I don't believe that all our foods should come out of packages. But I do think we should use the best available healthy processed foods to make cooking easier and food taste better. I take advantage of the good-tasting low-fat and low-sugar products found in any grocery store. My recipes are created for busy people like me, people who want to eat healthily and economically but who still want the food to satisfy their tastebuds. I don't expect any-one to visit out-of-the-way health food stores or find the time to cook beans from scratch—*because I don't!* Most of you can't grow fresh food in the backyard and many of you may not have access to farmers' markets or large supermarkets. I want to help you figure out realistic ways to make healthy eating a reality *wherever you live*, or you will not stick to a healthy lifestyle for long.

So if you've been swayed (by individuals or companies with vested interests or hidden agendas) into thinking that all processed foods are bad for you, you may want to reconsider your position. Or if you've been fooling yourself into believing that you *never* use processed foods but regularly reach for that healthy canned soup, stop playing games with yourself—you are using processed foods in a healthy way. And, if you're like me and use healthy processed foods in *moderation*, don't let anyone make you feel ashamed about including these products in your healthy lifestyle. Only *you* can decide what's best for *you* and your family's needs.

Part of living a healthy lifestyle is making those decisions and then getting on with life. Congratulations on choosing to live a healthy lifestyle, and let's celebrate together by sharing a piece of Healthy Exchanges pie that I've garnished with Cool Whip Lite!

JoAnna's Ten Commandments of Successful Cooking

A very important part of any journey is knowing where you are going and the best way to get there. If you plan and prepare before you start to cook, you should reach mealtime with foods to write home about!

1. **Read the entire recipe from start to finish** and be sure you understand the process involved. Check that you have all the equipment you will need *before* you begin.

2. **Check the ingredient list** and be sure you have *everything* and in the amounts required. Keep cooking sprays handy—while they're not listed as ingredients, I use them all the time (just a quick squirt!).

3. **Set out *all* the ingredients and equipment needed** to prepare the recipe on the counter near you *before* you start. Remember that old saying *A stitch in time saves nine*? It applies in the kitchen, too.

4. **Do as much advance preparation as possible** before actually cooking. Chop, cut, grate, or do whatever is needed to prepare the ingredients and have them ready before you start to mix. Turn the oven on at least ten min-

utes before putting food in to bake, to allow the oven to preheat to the proper temperature.

5. **Use a kitchen timer** to tell you when the cooking or baking time is up. Because stove temperatures vary slightly by manufacturer, you may want to set your timer for five minutes less than the suggested time just to prevent overcooking. Check the progress of your dish at that time, then decide if you need the additional minutes or not.

6. **Measure carefully.** Use glass measures for liquids and metal or plastic cups for dry ingredients. My recipes are based on standard measurements. Unless I tell you it's a scant or full cup, measure the cup level.

7. **For best results, follow the recipe instructions exactly.** Feel free to substitute ingredients that *don't tamper* with the basic chemistry of the recipe, but be sure to leave key ingredients alone. For example, you could substitute sugar-free instant chocolate pudding for sugar-free instant butterscotch pudding, but if you use a six-serving package when a four-serving package is listed in the ingredients, or you use instant when cook-and-serve is required, you won't get the right result.

8. **Clean up as you go.** It is much easier to wash a few items at a time than to face a whole counter of dirty dishes later. The same is true for spills on the counter or floor.

9. **Be careful about doubling or halving a recipe.** Though many recipes can be altered successfully to serve more or fewer people, *many cannot.* This is especially true when it comes to spices and liquids. If you try to double a recipe that calls for 1 teaspoon pumpkin pie spice, for example, and you double the spice, you may end up with a too-spicy taste. I usually suggest increasing spices or liquid by 1½ times when doubling a recipe. If it tastes a little bland to you, you can increase the spice to 1¾ times the original amount the next time you prepare the dish. Remember: You can always add more, but you can't take it out after it's stirred in.

The same is true with liquid ingredients. If you wanted to **triple** a recipe like my **Zach's Breakfast Muffins** because you were planning to serve a crowd, you might think you should use three times as much of every ingredient. Don't, or you could end up with a real mess! For the best possible result, **I recommend baking three batches** if you need three times the muffins, breads, or coffeecakes.

10. **Write your reactions next to each recipe once you've served it.** Yes, that's right, I'm giving you permission to write in this book. It's yours, after all. Ask yourself: Did everyone like it? Did you have to add another half teaspoon of chili seasoning to please your family, who like to live on the spicier side of the street? You may even want to rate the recipe on a scale of 1☆ to 4☆, depending on what you thought of it. (Four stars would be the top rating—and I hope you'll feel that way about many of my recipes.) Jotting down your comments while they are fresh in your mind will help you personalize the recipe to your own taste the next time you prepare it.

My Best Healthy Exchanges Tips and Tidbits

Measurements, General Cooking Tips, and Basic Ingredients

Sugar Substitutes

The word **moderation** best describes **my use of fats, sugar substitutes,** and **sodium** in these recipes. Wherever possible, I've used cooking spray for sautéing and for browning meats and vegetables. I also use reduced-calorie margarine and fat-free mayonnaise and salad dressings. Lean ground turkey *or* ground beef can be used in the recipes. Just be sure whatever you choose is at least *90 percent lean.*

I've also included **small amounts of sugar substitutes as the sweetening agent** in many of the recipes. I don't drink a hundred cans of soda a day or eat enough artificially sweetened foods in a 24-hour time period to be troubled by sugar substitutes. But if this is a concern of yours and you *do not* need to watch your sugar intake, you can always replace the sugar substitutes with processed sugar and the sugar-free products with regular ones.

I created my recipes knowing they would also be used by hypoglycemics, diabetics, and those concerned about triglycerides. If you choose to use sugar instead, be sure to count the additional calories.

A word of caution when cooking with **sugar substitutes**: Use **saccharin**-based sweeteners when **heating or baking**. In recipes that **don't require heat, aspartame** (known as NutraSweet) works well in uncooked dishes but leaves an aftertaste in baked products.

Sugar Twin is my first choice for a sugar substitute. If you can't find that, use **Sprinkle Sweet.** They measure like sugar, you can cook and bake with them, they're inexpensive, and they are easily poured from their boxes.

Many of my recipes for quick bread, muffins, and cakes include a package of sugar-free instant pudding mix, which is sweetenedwith NutraSweet. Yet we've been told that NutraSweet breaks down under heat. I'v tested my recipes again and again, and here's what I've found: baking with a NutraSweet product sold for home sweetening doesn't work, but baking with NutraSweet-sweetened instant pudding mixes turns out great. I choose not to question why this is, but continue to use these products in creating my Healthy Exchanges recipes.

How much sweetener is the right amount? I use pourable Sugar Twin, Brown Sugar Twin, and Sprinkle Sweet in my recipes because they measure just like sugar. What could be easier? I also use them because they work wonderfully in cooked and baked products.

If you are using a brand other than these, you need to check the package to figure out how much of your sweetener will equal what's called for in the recipe.

If you choose to use real sugar or brown sugar, then you would use the same amount the recipe lists for pourable Sugar Twin or Brown Sugar Twin.

You'll see that I list specific brands only when the recipe preparation involves heat. In a salad or other recipe that doesn't require cooking, I will list the ingredient as "sugar substitute to equal 2 tablespoons sugar." You can then use any sweetener you choose— Equal, Sweet'n Low, Sweet Ten, or any other aspartame-based sugar substitute. Just check the label so you'll be using the right amount to equal those 2 tablespoons of sugar. Or if you choose, you can use regular sugar.

With Healthy Exchanges recipes, the "sweet life" is the only life for me!

Pan Sizes

I'm often asked why I use an **8-by-8-inch baking dish** in my recipes. It's for portion control. If the recipe says it serves 4, just cut down the center, turn the dish, and cut again. Like magic, there's your serving. Also, if this is the only recipe you are preparing requiring an oven, the square dish fits into a tabletop toaster oven easily and energy can be conserved.

While many of my recipes call for an 8-by-8-inch baking dish, others ask for a 9-by-9-inch cake pan. If you don't have a 9-inch-square pan, is it all right to use your 8-inch dish instead? In most cases, the small difference in the size of these two pans won't significantly affect the finished product, so until you can get your hands on the right size pan, go ahead and use your baking dish.

However, since the 8-inch dish is usually made of glass, and the 9-inch cake pan is made of metal, you will want to adjust the baking temperature. If you're using a glass baking dish in a recipe that calls for a 9-inch pan, be sure to lower your baking temperature by 15 degrees *or* check your finished product at least 6 to 8 minutes before the specified baking time is over.

But it really is worthwhile to add a 9-by-9-inch pan to your collection, and if you're going to be baking lots of my Healthy Exchanges cakes, you'll definitely use it a lot. A cake baked in this pan will have a better texture, and the servings will be a little larger. Just think of it—an 8-by-8-inch pan produces 64 square inches of dessert, while a 9-by-9-inch pan delivers 81 square inches. Those 17 extra inches are too tasty to lose!

To make life even easier, **whenever a recipe calls for ounce measurements** (other than raw meats) I've included the closest cup equivalent. I need to use my scale daily when creating recipes, so I've measured for you at the same time.

Freezing Leftovers

Most of the recipes are for **4 to 8 servings.** If you don't have that many to feed, do what I do: freeze individual portions. Then all you have to do is choose something from the freezer and take it to work for lunch or have your evening meals prepared in advance for the week. In this way, I always have something on hand that is both good to eat and good for me.

Unless a recipe includes hard-boiled eggs, cream cheese, mayonnaise, or a raw vegetable or fruit, **the leftovers should freeze well**. (I've marked recipes that freeze well with the symbol of a **snowflake❆**.) This includes most of the cream pies. Divide any recipe into individual servings and freeze for your own TV dinners.

Another good idea is **cutting leftover pie into individual pieces and freezing each one separately** in a small Ziploc freezer bag. Once you've cut the pie into portions, place them on a cookie sheet and put it in the freezer for 15 minutes. That way, the creamy topping won't get smashed and your pie will keep its shape.

When you want to thaw a piece of pie for yourself, you don't have to thaw the whole pie. You can practice portion control at the same time, and it works really well for brown-bag lunches. Just pull a piece out of the freezer on your way to work and by lunchtime you will have a wonderful dessert waiting for you.

Why do I so often recommend freezing leftover desserts? One reason is that if you leave baked goods made with sugar substitute out on the counter for more than a day or two, they get moldy. Sugar is a preservative and retards the molding process. It's actually what's called an antimicrobial agent, meaning it works against microbes such as molds, bacteria, fungi, and yeasts that grow in foods and can cause food poisoning. Both sugar and salt work as antimicrobial agents to withdraw water from food. Since microbes can't grow without water, food protected in this way doesn't spoil.

So what do we do if we don't want our muffins to turn moldy, but we also don't want to use sugar because of the excess carbohydrates and calories? Freeze them! Just place each muffin or individually sliced bread serving into a Ziploc sandwich bag, seal, and toss into your freezer. Then, whenever you want one for a snack or a meal, you can choose to let it thaw naturally or "zap" it in the microwave. If you know that baked goods will be eaten within a day or two, packaging them in a sealed plastic container and storing in the refrigerator will do the trick.

Unless I specify **"covered" for simmering or baking**, prepare my recipes **uncovered**. Occasionally you will read a recipe that asks you to cover a dish for a time, then to uncover, so read the directions carefully to avoid confusion—and to get the best results.

Cooking Spray

Low-fat cooking spray is another blessing in a Healthy Exchanges kitchen. It's currently available in three flavors . . .

- **OLIVE OIL–FLAVORED** when cooking Mexican, Italian, or Greek dishes

- **BUTTER-FLAVORED** when the hint of butter is desired

- **REGULAR** for everything else.

A quick spray of butter-flavored makes air-popped popcorn a low-fat taste treat, or try it as a butter substitute on steaming hot corn on the cob. One light spray of the skillet when browning meat will convince you that you're using "old-fashioned fat," and a quick coating of the casserole dish before you add the ingredients will make serving easier and cleanup quicker.

Baking Times

Sometimes I give you a range as a **baking time**, such as 22 to 28 minutes. Why? Because every kitchen, every stove, and every chef's cooking technique are slightly different. On a hot and humid day in Iowa, the optimum cooking time won't be the same as on a cold, dry day. Some stoves bake hotter than the temperature setting indicates; other stoves bake cooler. Electric ovens are usually more temperamental than gas ovens. If you place your baking pan on a lower shelf, the temperature is warmer than if you place it on a higher shelf. If you stir the mixture more vigorously than I do, you could affect the required baking time by a minute or more.

The best way to gauge the heat of your particular oven is to purchase an oven temperature gauge that hangs in the oven. These can be found in any discount store or kitchen equipment store, and if you're going to be cooking and baking regularly, it's a good idea to own one. Set the oven to 350 degrees and when the oven indicates that it has reached that temperature, check the reading on the gauge. If it's less than 350 degrees, you know your oven cooks cooler, and you need to add a few minutes to the cooking time *or* set your oven at a higher temperature. If it's more than 350 degrees, then your oven is warmer and you need to subtract a few minutes from the cooking time. In any event, always treat the suggested baking time as approximate. Check on your baked product at the earliest suggested time. You can always continue baking a few minutes more if needed, but you can't unbake it once you've cooked it too long.

Miscellaneous Ingredients/Tips

I use reduced-sodium **canned chicken broth** in place of dry bouillon to lower the sodium content. The intended flavor is still present in the prepared dish. As a reduced-sodium beef broth is not currently available (at least not in DeWitt, Iowa), I use the canned regular beef broth. The sodium content is still lower than regular dry bouillon.

Whenever **cooked rice or pasta** is an ingredient, follow the package directions, but eliminate the salt and/or margarine called for. This helps lower the sodium and fat content. It tastes just fine; trust me on this.

Here's another tip: When **cooking rice or noodles**, why not cook extra "for the pot"? After you use what you need, store leftover rice in a covered container (where it will keep for a couple of days). With noodles like spaghetti or macaroni, first rinse and drain as usual, then measure out what you need. Put the leftovers in a bowl covered with water, then store in the refrigerator, covered, until they're needed. Then, measure out what you need, rinse and drain them, and they're ready to go.

Does your **pita bread** often tear before you can make a sandwich? Here's my tip to make them open easily: cut the bread in half, put the halves in the microwave for about 15 seconds, and they will open up by themselves. *Voilà!*

When **chunky salsa** is listed as an ingredient, I leave the degree of "heat" up to your personal taste. In our house, I'm considered a wimp. I go for the "mild" while Cliff prefers "extra-hot." How do we compromise? I prepare the recipe with mild salsa because he can always add a spoonful or two of the hotter version to his serving, but I can't enjoy the dish if it's too spicy for me.

Milk, Yogurt, and More

Take it from me—nonfat dry milk powder is great! I *do not* use it for drinking, but I *do* use it for cooking. Three good reasons why:

1. It is very **inexpensive**.

2. It does not **sour** because you use it only as needed. Store the box in your refrigerator or freezer and it will keep almost forever.

3. You can easily **add extra calcium** to just about any recipe without added liquid.

I consider nonfat dry milk powder one of Mother Nature's modern-day miracles of convenience. But do purchase a good national name brand (I like Carnation) and keep it fresh by proper storage.

I've said many times, "Give me my mixing bowl, my wire whisk, and a box of nonfat dry milk powder, and I can conquer the world!" Here are some of my favorite ways to use dry milk powder:

1. You can make a **pudding** with the nutrients of 2 cups skim milk, but the liquid of only 1¼ to 1½ cups by using ⅔ cup nonfat dry milk powder, a 4-serving package of sugar-free instant pudding, and the lesser amount of water. This makes the pudding taste much creamier and more like homemade. Also, pie filling made my way will set up in minutes. If company is knocking at your door, you can prepare a pie for them almost as fast as you can open the door and invite them in. And if by chance you have leftovers, the filling will not separate the way it does when you use the 2 cups of skim milk suggested on the package. (If you absolutely refuse to use this handy powdered milk, you can substitute skim milk in the amount of water I call for. Your pie won't be as creamy, and will likely get runny if you have leftovers.)

2. You can make your own **"sour cream"** by combining ¾ cup plain fat-free yogurt with ⅓ cup nonfat dry milk powder. What you did by doing this is fourfold: (1) The dry milk stabilizes the yogurt and keeps the whey from separating. (2) The dry milk slightly helps to cut the tartness of the yogurt.

(3) It's still virtually fat-free. (4) The calcium has been increased by 100 percent. Isn't it great how we can make that distant relative of sour cream a first kissin' cousin by adding the nonfat dry milk powder? Or, if you place 1 cup plain fat-free yogurt in a sieve lined with a coffee filter, and place the sieve over a small bowl and refrigerate for about 6 hours, you will end up with a very good alternative for sour cream. To **stabilize yogurt** when cooking or baking with it, just add 1 teaspoon cornstarch to every ¾ cup yogurt.

3. You can make **evaporated skim milk** by using ⅓ cup nonfat dry milk powder and ½ cup water for every ½ cup evaporated skim milk you need. This is handy to know when you want to prepare a recipe calling for evaporated skim milk and you don't have any in the cupboard. And if you are using a recipe that requires only 1 cup evaporated skim milk, you don't have to worry about what to do with the leftover milk in the can.

4. You can make **sugar-free and fat-free sweetened condensed milk** by using 1⅓ cups nonfat dry milk powder mixed with ½ cup cold water and microwaving on HIGH until mixture is hot but not boiling. Then stir in ½ cup Sprinkle Sweet or pourable Sugar Twin. Cover and chill at least 4 hours.

5. For any recipe that calls for **buttermilk**, you might want to try **JO's Buttermilk**: Blend 1 cup water and ⅔ cup nonfat dry milk powder (the nutrients of 2 cups of skim milk). It'll be thicker than this mixed-up milk usually is, because it's doubled. Add 1 teaspoon white vinegar and stir, then let it sit for at least ten minutes.

What else? Nonfat dry milk powder adds calcium without fuss to many recipes, and it can be stored for months in your refrigerator or freezer.

Soup Substitutes

One of my subscribers was looking for a way to further restrict salt intake and needed a substitute for **cream of mushroom soup**. For many of my recipes, I use Healthy Request Cream of Mushroom Soup, as it is a reduced-sodium product. The label suggests two servings per can, but I usually incorporate the soup into a recipe serving at least four. By doing this, I've reduced the sodium in the soup by half again.

But if you must restrict your sodium even more, try making my Healthy Exchanges **Creamy Mushroom Sauce.** Place 1½ cups evaporated skim milk and 3 tablespoons flour in a covered jar. Shake well and pour the mixture into a medium saucepan sprayed with butter-flavored cooking spray. Add ½ cup canned sliced mushrooms, rinsed and drained. Cook over medium heat, stirring often, until the mixture thickens. Add any seasonings of your choice. You can use this sauce in any recipe that calls for one 10¾-ounce can of cream of mushroom soup.

Why did I choose these proportions and ingredients?

- 1½ cups evaporated skim milk is the amount in one can.
- It's equal to three Skim Milk choices or exchanges.
- It's the perfect amount of liquid and flour for a medium cream sauce.
- 3 tablespoons flour is equal to one Bread/Starch choice or exchange.
- Any leftovers will reheat beautifully with a flour-based sauce, but not with a cornstarch base.
- The mushrooms are one Vegetable choice or exchange.
- This sauce is virtually fat-free, sugar-free, and sodium-free.

Proteins

Eggs

I use eggs in moderation. I enjoy the real thing on an average of three to four times a week. So, my recipes are calculated on using whole eggs. However, if you choose to use egg substitute in place of the egg, the finished product will turn out just fine and the fat grams per serving will be even lower than those listed.

If you like the look, taste, and feel of **hard-boiled eggs** in salads but haven't been using them because of the cholesterol in the yolk, I have a couple of alternatives for you. (1) Pour an 8-ounce carton of egg substitute into a medium skillet sprayed with cooking spray. Cover the skillet tightly and cook over low heat until the substitute is just set, about 10 minutes. Remove from heat and let set, still covered, for 10 minutes more. Uncover and cool completely. Chop the set mixture. This will make about 1 cup of chopped egg. (2) Even easier is to hard-boil "real eggs," toss the yolk away, and chop the white. Either way, you don't deprive yourself of the pleasure of egg in your salad.

In most recipes calling for **egg substitutes**, you can use 2 egg whites in place of the equivalent of 1 egg substitute. Just break the eggs open and toss the yolks away. I can hear some of you already saying, "But that's wasteful!" Well, take a look at the price on the egg substitute package (which usually has the equivalent of 4 eggs in it), then look at the price of a dozen eggs, from which you'd get the equivalent of 6 egg substitutes. Now, what's wasteful about that?

Meats

Whenever I include **cooked chicken** in a recipe, I use roasted white meat without skin. Whenever I include **roast beef or pork** in a recipe, I use the loin cuts because they are much leaner. However, most of the time, I do my roasting of all these meats at the local deli. I just ask for a chunk of their lean roasted meat, 6 or 8 ounces, and ask them not to slice it. When I get home, I cube or dice the meat and am ready to use it in my recipe. The reason I do this is three-fold: (1) I'm getting just the amount I need without leftovers; (2) I don't have the expense of heating the oven; and (3) I'm not throwing away the bone, gristle, and fat I'd be cutting off the meat. Overall, it is probably cheaper to "roast" it the way I do.

Did you know that you can make an acceptable meatloaf without using egg for the binding? Just replace every egg with ¼ cup of liquid. You could use beef broth, tomato sauce, even applesauce, to name just a few. For a meatloaf to serve 6, I always use 1 pound of extra-lean ground beef or turkey, 6 tablespoons of dried fine bread crumbs, and ¼ cup of the liquid, plus anything else healthy that strikes my fancy at the time. I mix well and place the mixture in an 8-by-8-inch baking dish or 9-by-5-inch loaf pan sprayed with cooking spray. Bake uncovered at 350 degrees for 35 to 50 minutes (depending on the added ingredients). You will never miss the egg.

Any time you are **browning ground meat** for a casserole and want to get rid of almost all the excess fat, just place the uncooked meat loosely in a plastic colander. Set the colander in a glass pie plate. Place in the microwave and cook on HIGH for 3 to 6 minutes (depending on the amount being browned), stirring often. Use as you would for any casserole. You can also chop up onions and brown them with the meat if you want.

Gravy

For **gravy** with all the "old time" flavor but without the extra fat, try this almost effortless way to prepare it. (It's almost as easy as opening up a store-bought jar.) Pour the juice off your roasted meat, then set the roast aside to "rest" for about 20 minutes. Place the juice in an uncovered cake pan or other large flat pan (we want the large air surface to speed up the cooling process) and put in the freezer until the fat congeals on top and you can skim it off. Or, if you prefer, use a skimming pitcher purchased at your kitchen gadget store. Either way, measure about 1½ cups skimmed broth and pour into a medium saucepan. Cook over medium heat until heated through, about 5 minutes. In a covered jar, combine ½ cup water or cooled potato broth with 3 tablespoons flour. Shake well. Pour the flour mixture into the warmed juice. Combine well using a wire whisk. Continue cooking until the gravy thickens, about 5 minutes. Season with salt and pepper to taste.

Why did I use flour instead of cornstarch? Because any leftovers will reheat nicely with the flour base and would not with a cornstarch base. Also, 3 tablespoons of flour works out to 1 Bread/Starch exchange. This virtually fat-free gravy makes about 2 cups, so you could spoon about ½ cup gravy on your low-fat mashed potatoes and only have to count your gravy as ¼ Bread/Starch exchange.

Fruits and Vegetables

If you want to enjoy a **"fruit shake"** with some pizzazz, just combine soda water and unsweetened fruit juice in a blender. Add crushed ice. Blend on HIGH until thick. Refreshment without guilt.

You'll see that many recipes use ordinary **canned vegetables.**

They're much cheaper than reduced-sodium versions, and once you rinse and drain them, the sodium is reduced anyway. I believe in saving money wherever possible so we can afford the best fat-free and sugar-free products as they come onto the market.

All three kinds of **vegetables—fresh, frozen, and canned—** have their place in a healthy diet. My husband, Cliff, hates the taste of frozen or fresh green beans, thinks the texture is all wrong, so I use canned green beans instead. In this case, canned vegetables have their proper place when I'm feeding my husband. If someone in your family has a similar concern, it's important to respond to it so everyone can be happy and enjoy the meal.

When I use **fruits or vegetables** like apples, cucumbers, and zucchini, I wash them really well and **leave the skin on.** It provides added color, fiber, and attractiveness to any dish. And, because I use processed flour in my cooking, I like to increase the fiber in my diet by eating my fruits and vegetables in their closest-to-natural state.

To help keep **fresh fruits and veggies fresh,** just give them a quick "shower" with lemon juice. The easiest way to do this is to pour purchased lemon juice into a kitchen spray bottle and store in the refrigerator. Then, every time you use fresh fruits or vegetables in a salad or dessert, simply give them a quick spray with your "lemon spritzer." You just might be amazed by how this little trick keeps your produce from turning brown so fast.

The next time you warm canned vegetables such as carrots or green beans, drain and heat the vegetables in ¼ cup beef or chicken broth. It gives a nice variation to an old standby. Here's a simple **white sauce** for vegetables and casseroles without added fat that can be made by spraying a medium saucepan with butter-flavored cooking spray. Place 1½ cups evaporated skim milk and 3 tablespoons flour in a covered jar. Shake well. Pour into the sprayed saucepan and cook over medium heat until thick, stirring constantly. Add salt and pepper to taste. You can also add ½ cup canned drained mushrooms and/or 3 ounces (¾ cup) shredded reduced-fat cheese. Continue cooking until the cheese melts.

Zip up canned or frozen green beans with **chunky salsa**: ½ cup salsa to 2 cups beans. Heat thoroughly. Chunky salsa also makes a wonderful dressing on lettuce salads. It only counts as a vegetable, so enjoy.

Another wonderful **South of the Border** dressing can be stirred up by using ½ cup of chunky salsa and ¼ cup fat-free ranch dressing. Cover and store in your refrigerator. Use as a dressing for salads or as a topping for baked potatoes.

Delightful Dessert Ideas

For a special treat that tastes anything but "diet," try placing **spreadable fruit** in a container and microwave for about 15 seconds. Then pour the melted fruit spread over a serving of nonfat ice cream or frozen yogurt. One tablespoon of spreadable fruit is equal to 1 Fruit choice or exchange. Some combinations to get you started are apricot over chocolate ice cream, strawberry over strawberry ice cream, or any flavor over vanilla.

Another way I use spreadable fruit is to make a delicious **topping for a cheesecake or angel food cake**. I take ½ cup fruit and ½ cup Cool Whip Lite and blend the two together with a teaspoon of coconut extract.

Here's a really **good topping** for the fall of the year. Place 1½ cups unsweetened applesauce in a medium saucepan or 4-cup glass measure. Stir in 2 tablespoons raisins, 1 teaspoon apple pie spice, and 2 tablespoons Cary's Sugar Free Maple Syrup. Cook over medium heat on the stovetop or microwave on HIGH until warm. Then spoon about ½ cup of the warm mixture over pancakes, French toast, or sugar- and fat-free vanilla ice cream. It's as close as you will get to guilt-free apple pie!

Do you love hot fudge sundaes as much as I do? Here's my secret for making **Almost Sinless Hot Fudge Sauce**. Just combine the contents of a 4-serving package of JELL-O sugar-free chocolate cook-and-serve pudding with ⅔ cup Carnation Nonfat Dry Milk Powder in a medium saucepan. Add 1¼ cups water. Cook over medium heat, stirring constantly with a wire whisk, until the mixture thickens and starts to boil. Remove from heat and stir in 1 teaspoon vanilla extract, 2 teaspoons reduced-calorie margarine, and ½ cup miniature marshmallows. This makes six ¼-cup servings. Any leftovers can be refrigerated and reheated later in the microwave. Yes, you can buy fat-free chocolate syrup nowadays, but have you checked the sugar content? For a ¼ cup serving of store-bought syrup (and you show me any true hot fudge sundae lover who would settle for less than ¼ cup) it clocks in at over 150 calories with 39 grams of sugar! Hershey's Lite Syrup, while better, still has 100 calories and 10 grams of sugar. But this "homemade" version costs you only 60 calories, less than ½ gram of fat, and just 6 grams of sugar for the same ¼-cup serving. For an occasional squirt on something where 1 teaspoon is enough, I'll use Hershey's Lite Syrup. But when I crave a hot fudge sundae, I scoop out some sugar- and fat-free ice cream, then spoon my Almost Sinless Hot Fudge Sauce over the top and smile with pleasure.

A quick yet tasty way to prepare **strawberries for shortcake** is to place about ¾ cup sliced strawberries, 2 tablespoons Diet Mountain Dew, and sugar substitute to equal ¼ cup sugar in a blender container. Process on BLEND until the mixture is smooth. Pour the mixture into a bowl. Add 1¼ cups sliced strawberries and mix well. Cover and refrigerate until ready to serve with shortcakes. This tastes just like the strawberry sauce I remember my mother making when I was a child.

Have you tried **thawing Cool Whip Lite** by stirring it? Don't! You'll get a runny mess and ruin the look and taste of your dessert. You can *never* treat Cool Whip Lite the same way you did regular Cool Whip because the "lite" version just doesn't contain enough fat. Thaw your Cool Whip Lite by placing it in your refrigerator at least two hours before you need to use it. When they took the excess fat out of Cool Whip to make it "lite," they replaced it with air. When you stir the living daylights out of it to hurry up the thawing, you also stir out the air. You also can't thaw your Cool Whip Lite in the microwave, or you'll end up with Cool Whip Soup!

Always have a thawed container of Cool Whip Lite in your refrigerator, as it keeps well for up to two weeks. It actually freezes and thaws and freezes and thaws again quite well, so if you won't be using it soon, you could refreeze your leftovers. Just remember to take it out a few hours before you need it, so it'll be creamy and soft and ready to use.

Remember, anytime you see the words "fat-free" or "reduced-fat" on the labels of cream cheese, sour cream, or whipped topping, handle them gently. The fat has been replaced by air or water, and the product has to be treated with special care.

How can you **frost an entire pie with just ½ cup of whipped topping?** First, don't use an inexpensive brand. I use Cool Whip Lite or La Creme Lite. Make sure the topping is fully thawed. Always spread from the center to the sides using a rubber spatula. This way, ½ cup topping will cover an entire pie. Remember, the operative word is *frost,* not pile the entire container on top of the pie!

Another trick I often use is to include tiny amounts of "real people" food, such as coconut, but extend the flavor by using extracts. Try it—you will be surprised by how little of the real thing you can use and still feel you are not being deprived.

If you are preparing a pie filling that has ample moisture, just line the bottom of a 9-by-9-inch cake pan with **graham crackers**. Pour the filling over the top of the crackers. Cover and refrigerate until the moisture has enough time to soften the crackers. Overnight is best. This eliminates the added **fats and sugars of a piecrust.**

One of my readers provided a smart and easy way to enjoy a **two-crust pie** without all the fat that usually comes along with those two crusts. Just use one Pillsbury refrigerated piecrust. Let it set at room temperature for about 20 minutes. Cut the crust in half on the folded line. Gently roll each half into a ball. Wipe your counter with a wet cloth and place a sheet of wax paper on it. Put one of the balls on the wax paper, then cover with another piece of wax paper, and roll it out with your rolling pin. Carefully remove the wax paper on one side and place that side into your 8- or 9-inch pie plate. Fill with your usual pie filling, then repeat the process for the top crust. Bake as usual. Enjoy!

When you are preparing a pie that uses a purchased piecrust, simply tear out the paper label on the plastic cover (but do check it for a coupon good on a future purchase) and turn the cover upside down over the prepared pie. You now have a cover that protects your beautifully garnished pie from having anything fall on top of it. It makes the pie very portable when it's your turn to bring dessert to a get-together.

Did you know you can make your own **fruit-flavored yogurt?** Mix 1 tablespoon of any flavor of spreadable fruit spread with ¾ cup plain yogurt. It's every bit as tasty and much cheaper. You can also make your own **lemon yogurt** by combining 3 cups plain fat-free yogurt with 1 tub Crystal Light lemonade powder. Mix well, cover, and store in the refrigerator. I think you will be pleasantly surprised by the ease, cost, and flavor of this "made from scratch" calcium-rich treat. P.S.: You can make any flavor you like by using any of the Crystal Light mixes—Cranberry? Iced Tea? You decide.

Other Smart Substitutions

Many people have inquired about **substituting applesauce and artificial sweetener for butter and sugar**, but what if you aren't satisfied with the result? One woman wrote to me about a recipe for her grandmother's cookies that called for 1 cup of butter and 1½ cups of sugar. Well, any recipe that depends on as much butter and sugar as this one does is generally not a good candidate for "healthy exchanges." The original recipe needed a large quantity of fat to produce a crisp cookie just like Grandma made.

Applesauce can often be used instead of vegetable oil, but generally doesn't work well as a replacement for butter, margarine, or lard. If a recipe calls for ½ cup vegetable oil or less and your recipe is for a bar cookie, quick bread, muffin, or cake mix, you can try substituting an equal amount of unsweetened applesauce. If the recipe calls for more, try using ½ cup applesauce and the rest oil. You're cutting down the fat but shouldn't end up with a taste disaster! This "applesauce shortening" works great in many recipes, but so far I haven't been able to figure out a way to deep-fat fry with it!

Another rule for healthy substitution: Up to ½ cup sugar or less can be replaced by *an artificial sweetener that can withstand the heat of baking*, like pourable Sugar Twin or Sprinkle Sweet. If it requires more than ½ cup sugar, cut the amount needed by 75 percent and use ½ cup sugar substitute and sugar for the rest. Other options: reduce the butter and sugar by 25 percent and see if the finished product still satisfies you in taste and appearance. Or, make the cookies just like Grandma did, realizing they are part of your family's holiday tradition. Enjoy a *moderate* serving of a couple of cookies once or twice during the season, and just forget about them the rest of the year.

Did you know that you can replace the fat in many quick breads, muffins, and shortcakes with **fat-free mayonnaise** or **fat-free sour cream?** This can work if the original recipe doesn't call for a lot of fat *and* sugar. If the recipe is truly fat and sugar dependent, such as traditional sugar cookies, cupcakes, or pastries, it won't work. Those recipes require the large amounts of sugar and fat to make love in the dark of the oven to produce a tender finished product. But if you have a favorite quick bread that doesn't call for a lot of sugar or fat, why don't you give one of these substitutes a try?

If you enjoy beverage mixes like those from Alba, here are my Healthy Exchanges versions:

For **chocolate flavored,** use ⅓ cup nonfat dry milk powder and 2 tablespoons Nestlé Sugar-Free Chocolate Flavored Quik. Mix well and use as usual. Or, use ⅓ cup nonfat dry milk powder, 1 teaspoon unsweetened cocoa, and sugar substitute to equal 3 tablespoons sugar. Mix well and use as usual.

For **vanilla flavored,** use ⅓ cup nonfat dry milk powder, sugar substitute to equal 2 tablespoons sugar, and add 1 teaspoon vanilla extract when adding liquid.

For **strawberry flavored,** use ⅓ cup nonfat dry milk powder, sugar substitute to equal 2 tablespoons sugar, and add 1 teaspoon strawberry extract and 3–4 drops red food coloring when adding liquid.

Each of these makes one packet of drink mix. If you need to double the recipe, double everything but the extract. Use 1½ teaspoons of extract or it will be too strong. Use 1 cup cold water with one recipe mix to make a glass of flavored milk. If you want to make a shake, combine the mix, water, and 3–4 ice cubes in your blender, then process on BLEND till smooth.

A handy tip when making **healthy punch** for a party: Prepare a few extra cups of your chosen drink, freeze it in cubes in a couple of ice trays, then keep your punch from "watering down" by cooling it with punch cubes instead.

What should you do if you can't find the product listed in a Healthy Exchanges recipe? You can substitute in some cases—use Lemon JELL-O if you can't find Hawaiian Pineapple, for example. But if you're determined to track down the product you need, and your own store manager hasn't been able to order it for you, why not use one of the new online grocers and order exactly what you need, no matter where you live. Try **http://www.netgrocer.com.**

Not all low-fat cooking products are interchangeable, as one of my readers recently discovered when she tried to cook pancakes on her griddle using I Can't Believe It's Not Butter! spray—and they stuck! This butter-flavored spray is wonderful for a quick squirt on air-popped popcorn or corn on the cob, and it's great for topping your pancakes once they're cooked. In fact, my tastebuds have to check twice because it tastes so much like real butter! (And this is high praise from someone who once thought butter was the most perfect food ever created.)

But I Can't Believe It's Not Butter! doesn't work well for sautéing or browning. After trying to fry an egg with it and cooking up a disaster, I knew this product had its limitations. So I decided to continue using Pam or Weight Watchers butter-flavored cooking spray whenever I'm browning anything in a skillet or on a griddle.

Many of my readers have reported difficulty finding a product I use in many recipes: JELL-O cook-and-serve puddings. I have three suggestions for those of you with this problem:

1. **Work with your grocery store manager to get this product into your store**, and then make sure you and everyone you know buy it by the bagful! Products that sell well are reordered and kept in stock, especially with today's computerized cash registers that record what's purchased. You may also want to write or call Kraft General Foods and ask for their help. They can be reached at (800) 431-1001 weekdays from 9 A.M. to 4 P.M. (EST).

2. **You can prepare the recipe that calls for cook-and-serve pudding by using instant pudding of the same flavor.** Yes, that's right, you **can** cook with the instant when making my recipes. The finished product won't be quite as wonderful, but still at least a 3 on a 4-star scale. You can never do the opposite—never use cook-and-serve in a recipe that calls for instant! One time at a cooking demonstration, I could not understand why my Blueberry Mountain Cheesecake never did set up. Then I spotted the box in the trash and noticed I'd picked the wrong type of pudding mix. Be careful—the boxes are both blue, but the instant has pudding on a silver spoon, and the cook-and-serve has a stream of milk running down the front into a bowl with a wooden spoon.

3. **You can make JO's Sugar-Free Vanilla Cook-and-Serve Pudding Mix instead of using JELL-O's.** Here's my recipe:

2 tablespoons cornstarch, ½ cup pourable Sugar Twin or Sprinkle Sweet, ⅔ cup Carnation Nonfat Dry Milk Powder, 1½ cups water, 2 teaspoons vanilla extract, and 4 to 5 drops yellow food coloring. Combine all this in a medium saucepan and cook over medium heat, stirring constantly, until the mixture comes to a full boil and thickens. This is for basic cooked sugar-free vanilla pudding. For a chocolate version, the recipe is 2 tablespoons cornstarch, ¼ cup pourable Sugar Twin or Sprinkle Sweet, 2 tablespoons Nestlé's Sugar-Free Chocolate Flavored Quik, 1½ cups water, and 1 teaspoon vanilla extract. Follow the same cooking instructions as for the vanilla.

If you're preparing this as part of a recipe that also calls for adding a package of gelatin, just stir that into the mix.

Adapting a favorite family cake recipe? Here's something to try: Replace an egg and oil in the original with ⅓ cup plain fat-free yogurt and ¼ cup fat-free mayonnaise. Blend these two ingredients with your liquids in a separate bowl, then add the yogurt mixture to the flour mixture and mix gently just to combine. (You don't want to overmix or you'll release the gluten in the batter and end up with a tough batter.)

Want a tasty coffee creamer without all the fat? You could use Carnation's Fat Free Coffee-mate, which is 10 calories per teaspoon, but if you drink several cups a day with several teaspoons each, that adds up quickly to nearly 100 calories a day! Why not try my version? It's not quite as creamy, but it is good. Simply combine ⅓ cup Carnation Nonfat Dry Milk Powder and ¼ cup pourable Sugar Twin. Cover and store in your cupboard or refrigerator. At 3 calories per teaspoon, you can enjoy three teaspoons for less than the calories of one teaspoon of the purchased variety.

Some Helpful Hints

Sugar-free puddings and gelatins are important to many of my recipes, but if you prefer to avoid sugar substitutes, you could still prepare the recipes with regular puddings or gelatins. The calories would be higher, but you would still be cooking low-fat.

When a recipe calls for **chopped nuts** (and you only have whole ones), who wants to dirty the food processor just for a couple of tablespoonsful? You could try to chop them using your cutting board, but be prepared for bits and pieces to fly all over the kitchen. I use "Grandma's food processor." I take the biggest nuts I can find, put them in a small glass bowl, and chop them into chunks just the right size using a metal biscuit cutter.

A quick hint about **reduced-fat peanut butter:** Don't store it in the refrigerator. Because the fat has been reduced, it won't spread as easily when it's cold. Keep it in your cupboard and a little will spread a lot further.

Crushing **graham crackers** for topping? A self-seal sandwich bag works great!

If you have a **leftover muffin** and are looking for something a little different for breakfast, you can make a "**breakfast sundae.**" Crumble the muffin into a cereal bowl. Sprinkle a serving of fresh fruit over it and top with a couple of tablespoons of plain fat-free yogurt sweetened with sugar substitute and your choice of extract. The thought of it just might make you jump out of bed with a smile on your face. (Speaking of muffins, did you know that if you fill the unused muffin wells with water when baking muffins, you help ensure more even baking and protect the muffin pan at the same time?) Another muffin hint: Lightly spray the inside of paper baking cups with butter-flavored cooking spray before spooning the muffin batter into them. Then you won't end up with paper clinging to your fresh-baked muffins.

The secret of making **good meringues** without sugar is to use 1 tablespoon of Sprinkle Sweet or pourable Sugar Twin for every egg white, and a small amount of extract. Use ½ to 1 teaspoon for the batch. Almond, vanilla, and coconut are all good choices. Use the same amount of cream of tartar you usually do. Bake the meringue in the same old way. Even if you can't eat sugar, you can enjoy a healthy meringue pie when it's prepared the *Healthy Exchanges Way*. (Remember that egg whites whip up best at room temperature.)

Try **storing your Bisquick Reduced Fat Baking Mix** in the freezer. It won't freeze, and it *will* stay fresh much longer. (It works for coffee, doesn't it?)

If you lightly **spray the inside of paper baking cups** with butter-flavored cooking spray before spooning the muffin batter into them, you won't end up with "clinging paper" on your fresh-baked muffins. If you love muffins as much as I do, but hate washing muffin tins as much as I do, you'll agree this idea is worth its weight in muffin batter!

If you've ever wondered about **changing ingredients** in one of my recipes, the answer is that some things can be changed to suit your family's tastes, but others should not be tampered with. **Don't change:** the amount of flour, bread crumbs, reduced-fat baking mix, baking soda, baking powder, liquid, or dry milk powder. And if I include a small amount of salt, it's necessary for the recipe to turn out correctly. **What you can change:** an extract flavor (if you don't like coconut, choose vanilla or almond instead); a spreadable fruit flavor; the type of fruit in a pie filling (but be careful about substituting fresh for frozen and vice versa—sometimes it works but it may not); the flavor of pudding or gelatin. As long as package sizes and amounts are the same, go for it. It will never hurt my feelings if you change a recipe, so please your family—don't worry about me!

Because I always say that "good enough" isn't good enough for me anymore, here's a way to make your cup of **fat-free and sugar-free hot cocoa** more special. After combining the hot chocolate mix and hot water, stir in ½ teaspoon vanilla extract and a light sprinkle of cinnamon. If you really want to feel decadent, add a tablespoon of Cool Whip Lite. Isn't life grand?

If you must limit your sugar intake, but you love the idea of sprinkling **powdered sugar** on dessert crepes or burritos, here's a pretty good substitute: Place 1 cup Sprinkle Sweet or pourable Sugar Twin and 1 teaspoon cornstarch in a blender container, then cover and process on HIGH until the mixture resembles powdered sugar in texture, about 45 to 60 seconds. Store in an airtight container and use whenever you want a dusting of "powdered sugar" on any dessert.

Want my "almost instant" pies to set up even more quickly? Do as one of my readers does: freeze your Keebler piecrusts. Then, when you stir up one of my pies and pour the filling into the frozen crust, it sets up within seconds.

Some of my "island-inspired" recipes call for **rum or brandy extracts**, which provide the "essence" of liquor without the real thing. I'm a teetotaler by choice, so I choose not to include real liquor in any of my recipes. They're cheaper than liquor and you won't feel the need to shoo your kids away from the goodies. If you prefer not to use liquor extracts in your cooking, you can always substitute vanilla extract.

Some Healthy Cooking Challenges and How I Solved 'Em

When you stir up one of my pie fillings, do you ever have a problem with **lumps?** Here's an easy solution for all you "careful" cooks out there. Lumps occur when the pudding starts to set up before you can get the dry milk powder incorporated into the mixture. I always advise you to dump, pour, and stir fast with that wire whisk, letting no more than 30 seconds elapse from beginning to end.

But if you are still having problems, you can always combine the dry milk powder and the water in a separate bowl before adding the pudding mix and whisking quickly. Why don't I suggest this right from the beginning? Because that would mean an extra dish to wash every time—and you know I hate to wash dishes!

With a little practice and a light touch, you should soon get the hang of my original method. But now you've got an alternative way to lose those lumps!

I love the chemistry of foods and so I've gotten great pleasure from analyzing what makes fat-free products tick. By dissecting these "miracle" products, I've learned how to make them work best. They require different handling than the high-fat products we're used to, but if treated properly, these slimmed-down versions can produce delicious results!

Fat-free sour cream: This product is wonderful on a hot baked potato, but have you noticed that it tends to be much gummier than regular sour cream? If you want to use it in a stroganoff dish or baked product, you must stir a tablespoon or two of skim milk into the fat-free sour cream before adding it to other ingredients.

Cool Whip Free: When the fat went out of the formula, air was stirred in to fill the void. So, if you stir it too vigorously, you release the air and *decrease* the volume. Handle it with kid gloves—gently. Since the manufacturer forgot to ask for my input, I'll share with you how to make it taste almost the same as it used to. Let the container thaw in the refrigerator, then ever so gently stir in 1 teaspoon vanilla extract. Now, put the lid back on and enjoy it a tablespoon at a time, the same way you did Cool Whip Lite.

Fat-free cream cheese: When the fat was removed from this product, water replaced it. So don't ever use an electric mixer on the fat-free version, or you risk releasing the water and having your finished product look more like dip than cheesecake! Stirring it gently with a sturdy spoon in a glass bowl with a handle will soften it just as much as it needs to be. And don't be alarmed if the cream cheese gets caught in your wire whisk when you start combining the pudding mix and other ingredients. Just keep knocking it back down into the bowl by hitting the whisk against the rim of the bowl, and as you continue blending, it will soften even more and drop off the whisk. When it's time to pour the filling into your crust, your whisk shouldn't have anything much clinging to it.

Reduced-fat margarine: Again, the fat was replaced by water. If you try to use the reduced-fat kind in your cookie recipe spoon for spoon, you will end up with a cake-like cookie instead of the crisp kind most of us enjoy. You have to take into consideration that some water will be released as the product bakes. Use less liquid than the recipe calls for (when re-creating family recipes *only*—I've figured this into Healthy Exchanges recipes). And never, never, never use fat-*free* margarine and expect anyone to ask for seconds!

Homemade or Store-Bought?

I've been asked which is better for you: homemade from scratch, or purchased foods. My answer is *both!* Each has a place in a healthy lifestyle, and what that place is has everything to do with you.

Take **piecrusts**, for instance. If you love spending your spare time in the kitchen preparing foods, and you're using low-fat, low-sugar, and reasonably low sodium ingredients, go for it! But if, like so many people, your time is limited and you've learned to read labels, you could be better off using purchased foods.

I know that when I prepare a pie (and I experiment with a couple of pies each week, because this is Cliff's favorite dessert), I use a purchased crust. Why? Mainly because I can't make a good-tasting piecrust that is lower in fat than the brands I use. Also, purchased piecrusts fit my rule of "If it takes longer to fix than to eat, forget it!"

I've checked the nutrient information for the purchased piecrusts against recipes for traditional and "diet" piecrusts, using my computer software program. The purchased crust calculated lower in both fat and calories! I have tried some low-fat and low-sugar recipes, but they just didn't spark my taste buds, or were so complicated you needed an engineering degree just to get the crust in the pie plate.

I'm very happy with the purchased piecrusts in my recipes, because the finished product rarely, if ever, has more than 30 percent of total calories coming from fats. I also believe that we have to prepare foods our families and friends will eat with us on a regular basis and not feel deprived, or we've wasted time, energy, and money.

I could use a purchased "lite" **pie filling**, but instead I make my own. Here I can save both fat and sugar, and still make the filling almost as fast as opening a can. The bottom line: Know what you have to spend when it comes to both time and fat/sugar calories, then make the best decision you can for you and your family. And don't go without an occasional piece of pie because you think it isn't *necessary*. A delicious pie prepared in a healthy way is one of the simple pleasures of life. It's a little thing, but it can make all the difference between just getting by with the bare minimum and living a full and healthy lifestyle.

I'm sure you'll add to this list of cooking tips as you begin preparing Healthy Exchanges recipes and discover how easy it can be to adapt your own favorite recipes using these ideas and your own common sense.

A Peek into My Pantry and My Favorite Brands

Everyone asks me what foods I keep on hand and what brands I use. There are lots of good products on the grocery shelves today—many more than we dreamed about even a year or two ago. And I can't wait to see what's out there twelve months from now. The following are my staples and, where appropriate, my favorites *at this time*. I feel these products are healthier, tastier, easy to get— and deliver the most flavor for the least amount of fat, sugar, or calories. If you find others you like as well *or better*, please use them. This is only a guide to make your grocery shopping and cooking easier. (You'll note that I've supplied you with my entire current list of favorites, even though some products are not used in any of my recipes. I hope this makes your shopping easier.)

> Fat-free plain yogurt (*Yoplait or Dannon*)
> Nonfat dry milk powder (*Carnation*)
> Evaporated skim milk (*Carnation*)
> Skim milk
> Fat-free cottage cheese
> Fat-free cream cheese (*Philadelphia*)
> Fat-free mayonnaise (*Kraft*)
> Fat-free salad dressings (*Kraft*)
> Fat-free sour cream (*Land O Lakes*)
> Reduced-calorie margarine (*Weight Watchers, Promise, or Smart Beat*)

Cooking spray
  Olive oil–flavored and regular (*Pam*)
  Butter-flavored for sautéing (*Pam or Weight Watchers*)
  Butter-flavored for spritzing *after* cooking (*I Can't Believe It's Not Butter!*)
Vegetable oil (*Puritan Canola Oil*)
Reduced-calorie whipped topping (*Cool Whip Lite or Cool Whip Free*)
Sugar substitute
  if no heating is involved (*Equal*)
  if heating is required
    white (*pourable Sugar Twin or Sprinkle Sweet*)
    brown (*Brown Sugar Twin*)
Sugar-free gelatin and pudding mixes (*JELL-O*)
Baking mix (*Bisquick Reduced Fat*)
Pancake mix (*Aunt Jemima Reduced Calorie*)
Reduced-calorie pancake syrup (*Cary's Sugar Free*)
Parmesan cheese (*Kraft fat-free*)
Reduced-fat cheese (*Kraft 2% Reduced Fat*)
Shredded frozen potatoes (*Mr. Dell's*)
Spreadable fruit spread (*Smucker's, Welch's, or Knott's Berry Farm*)
Peanut butter (*Peter Pan reduced-fat, Jif reduced-fat, or Skippy reduced-fat*)
Chicken broth (*Healthy Request*)
Beef broth (*Swanson*)
Tomato sauce (*Hunt's—plain, Italian, or chili*)
Canned soups (*Healthy Request*)
Tomato juice (*Campbell's Reduced-Sodium*)
Ketchup (*Heinz Light Harvest or Healthy Choice*)
Purchased piecrust
  unbaked (*Pillsbury—from dairy case*)
  graham cracker, butter flavored, or chocolate flavored (*Keebler*)
Crescent rolls (*Pillsbury Reduced Fat*)
Pastrami and corned beef (*Carl Buddig Lean*)
Luncheon meats (*Healthy Choice or Oscar Mayer*)
Ham (*Dubuque 97% fat-free and reduced-sodium or Healthy Choice*)

Frankfurters and kielbasa sausage (*Healthy Choice*)
Canned white chicken, packed in water (*Swanson*)
Canned tuna, packed in water (*Starkist or Chicken of the Sea*)
90-95 percent lean ground turkey and beef
Soda crackers (*Nabisco Fat-Free*)
Reduced-calorie bread—40 calories per slice or less
Hamburger buns—80 calories each (*Less*)
Rice—instant, regular, brown, and wild
Instant potato flakes (*Betty Crocker Potato Buds*)
Noodles, spaghetti, and macaroni
Salsa (*Chi-Chi's Mild Chunky*)
Pickle relish—dill, sweet, and hot dog
Mustard—Dijon, prepared, and spicy
Unsweetened apple juice
Unsweetened applesauce
Fruit—fresh, frozen (no sugar added), or canned in juice
Vegetables—fresh, frozen, or canned
Spices—JO's Spices
Lemon and lime juice (in small plastic fruit-shaped bottles
    found in the produce section)
Instant fruit beverage mixes (*Crystal Light*)
Dry dairy beverage mixes (*Nestlé Quik*)
"Ice cream" (*Wells' Blue Bunny sugar- and fat-free*)

The items on my shopping list are everyday foods found in just about any grocery store in America. But all are as low in fat, sugar, calories, and sodium as I can find—and still taste good! I can make any recipe in my cookbooks and newsletters as long as I have my cupboards and refrigerator stocked with these items. Whenever I use the last of any one item, I just make sure I pick up another supply the next time I'm at the store.

If your grocer does not stock these items, why not ask if they can be ordered on a trial basis? If the store agrees to do so, be sure to tell your friends to stop by, so that sales are good enough to warrant restocking the new products. Competition for shelf space is fierce, so only products that sell well stay around.

Shopping the Healthy Exchanges Way

Sometimes, as part of a cooking demonstration, I take the group on a field trip to the nearest supermarket. There's no better place to share my discoveries about which healthy products taste best, which are best for you, and which healthy products don't deliver enough taste to include in my recipes.

While I'd certainly enjoy accompanying you to your neighborhood store, we'll have to settle for a field trip *on paper*. I've tasted and tried just about every fat- and sugar-free product on the market, but so many new ones keep coming all the time, you're going to have to learn to play detective on your own. I've turned label reading into an art, but often the label doesn't tell me everything I need to know.

Sometimes you'll find, as I have, that the product with *no* fat doesn't provide the taste satisfaction you require; other times, a no-fat or low-fat product just doesn't cook up the same way as the original product. And some foods, including even the leanest meats, can't eliminate *all* the fat. That's okay, though—a healthy diet should include anywhere from 15 to 25 percent of total calories from fat on any given day.

Take my word for it—your supermarket is filled with lots of delicious foods that can and should be part of your healthy diet for life. Come, join me as we check it out on the way to the checkout!

Before I buy anything at the store, I read the label carefully: I check the total fat plus the saturated fat; I look to see how many calories are in a realistic serving, and I say to myself, Would I eat that much—or would I eat more? I look at the sodium and I look at the total carbohydrates. I like to check those ingredients because I'm cooking for diabetics and heart patients too. And I check the total calories from fat.

Remember that 1 fat gram equals 9 calories, while 1 protein or 1 carbohydrate gram equals 4 calories.

A wonderful new product is I Can't Believe It's Not Butter! spray, with zero calories and zero grams of fat in five squirts. It's great for your air-popped popcorn. As for **light margarine spread**, beware—most of the fat-free brands don't melt on toast, and they don't taste very good either, so I just leave them on the shelf. For the few times I do use a light margarine I tend to buy Smart Beat Ultra, Promise Ultra, or Weight Watchers Light Ultra. The number-one ingredient in them is water. I occasionally use the light margarine in cooking, but I don't really put margarine on my toast anymore. I use apple butter or make a spread with fat-free cream cheese mixed with a little spreadable fruit instead.

So far, Pillsbury hasn't released a reduced-fat **crescent roll**, so you'll only get one crescent roll per serving from me. I usually make eight of the rolls serve twelve by using them for a crust. The house brands may be lower in fat but they're usually not as good flavor-wise—and they don't quite cover the pan when you use them to make a crust. If you're going to use crescent rolls with lots of other stuff on top, then a house brand might be fine.

The Pillsbury French Loaf makes a wonderful **pizza crust** and fills a giant jelly-roll pan. One-fifth of this package "costs" you only 1 gram of fat (and I don't even let you have that much!). Once you use this for your pizza crust, you will never go back to anything else instead. I use it to make calzones too.

I use only Philadelphia fat-free **cream cheese** because it has the best consistency. I've tried other brands, but I wasn't happy with them. Healthy Choice makes lots of great products, but their cream cheese just doesn't work as well with my recipes.

Let's move to the **cheese** aisle. My preferred brand is Kraft 2% Reduced Fat Shredded Cheeses. I will not use the fat-free versions because *they don't melt*. I would gladly give up sugar and fat, but I will not give up flavor. This is a happy compromise. I use the reduced-fat version, I use less, and I use it where your eyes "eat" it, on top of the recipe. So you walk away satisfied and with a finished product that's very low in fat. If you want to make grilled-cheese sandwiches for your kids, use the Kraft reduced-fat cheese slices, and they'll taste exactly like the ones they're used to. The fat-free will not.

Dubuque's Extra-Lean Reduced-Sodium **ham** tastes wonderful, reduces the sodium as well as the fat, and gives you a larger serving. Don't be fooled by products called turkey ham; they may *not* be lower in fat than a very lean pork product. Here's one label as an example: I checked a brand of turkey ham called Genoa. It gives you a 2-ounce serving for 70 calories and 3½ grams of fat. The Dubuque extra-lean ham, made from pork, gives you a 3-ounce serving for 90 calories, but only 2½ grams of fat. *You get more food and less fat.*

Frozen dinners can be expensive and high in sodium, but it's smart to have two or three in the freezer as a backup when your best-laid plans go awry and you need to grab something on the run. It's not a good idea to rely on them too much—what if you can't get to the store to get them, or you're short on cash? The sodium can be high in some of them because they often replace the fat with salt, so be sure to read the labels. Also ask yourself if the serving is enough to satisfy you; for many of us, it's not.

Egg substitute is expensive, and probably not necessary unless you're cooking for someone who has to worry about every bit of cholesterol in his or her diet. If you occasionally have a fried egg or an omelet, *use the real egg.* For cooking, you can usually substitute two egg whites for one whole egg. Most of the time it won't make any difference, but check your recipe carefully.

Healthy frozen desserts are hard to find except for the Weight Watchers brands. I've always felt that their portions are so small, and for their size still pretty high in fat and sugar. (This is one of the reasons I think I'll be successful marketing my frozen desserts someday. After Cliff tasted one of my earliest healthy pies—and licked the plate clean—he remarked that if I ever opened a restaurant, people would keep coming back for my desserts alone!) Keep an eye out for fat-free or very low-fat frozen yogurt or sorbet products. Even Häagen-Dazs, which makes some of the highest-fat-content ice cream, now has a fat-free fruit sorbet pop out that's pretty good. I'm sure there will be more before too long.

You have to be realistic: What are you willing to do, and what are you *not* willing to do? Let's take **bread**, for example. Some people just have to have the real thing—rye bread with caraway seeds or a whole-wheat version with bits of bran in it.

I prefer to use reduced-calorie bread because I like a *real* sandwich. This way, I can have two slices of bread and it counts as only one Bread/Starch exchange.

How I Shop for Myself

I always keep my kitchen stocked with my basic staples; that way, I can go to the cupboard and create new recipes anytime I'm inspired. I hope you will take the time (and allot the money) to stock your cupboards with items from the staples list, so you can enjoy developing your own healthy versions of family favorites without making extra trips to the market.

I'm always on the lookout for new products sitting on the grocery shelf. When I spot something I haven't seen before, I'll usually grab it, glance at the front, then turn it around and read the label carefully. I call it looking at the "promises" (the "come-on" on the front of the package) and then at the "warranty" (the ingredients list and the label on the back).

If it looks as good on the back as it does on the front, I'll say okay and either create a recipe on the spot or take it home for when I do think of something to do with it. Picking up a new product is just about the only time I buy something not on my list.

The items on my shopping list are normal, everyday foods, but as low-fat and low-sugar (*while still tasting good*) as I can find. I can make any recipe in this book as long as these staples are on my shelves. After using these products for a couple of weeks, you will find it becomes routine to have them on hand. And I promise you, I really don't spend any more at the store now than I did a few years ago when I told myself I couldn't afford some of these items. Back then, of course, plenty of unhealthy, high-priced snacks I really didn't need somehow made the magic leap from the grocery shelves into my cart. Who was I kidding?

Yes, you often have to pay a little more for fat-free or low-fat products, including meats. But since I frequently use a half pound of meat to serve four to six people, your cost per serving will be much lower.

Try adding up what you were spending before on chips and cookies, premium-brand ice cream, and fatty cuts of meat, and you'll soon see that we've *streamlined* your shopping cart, and taken the weight off your pocketbook as well as your hips!

Remember, your good health is *your* business—but it's big business too. Write to the manufacturers of products you and your family enjoy but feel are just too high in fat, sugar, or sodium to be part of your new healthy lifestyle. Companies are spending millions of dollars to respond to consumers' concerns about food products, and I bet that in the next few years, you'll discover fat-free and low-fat versions of nearly every product piled high on your supermarket shelves!

The Healthy Exchanges Kitchen

You might be surprised to discover I still don't have a massive test kitchen stocked with every modern appliance and handy gadget ever made. The tiny galley kitchen where I first launched Healthy Exchanges has room for only one person at a time, but it never stopped me from feeling the sky's the limit when it comes to seeking out great healthy taste!

Because storage is at such a premium in my kitchen, I don't waste space with equipment I don't really need. Here's a list of what I consider worth having. If you notice serious gaps in your equipment, you can probably find most of what you need at a local discount store or garage sale. If your kitchen is equipped with more sophisticated appliances, don't feel guilty about using them. Enjoy every appliance you can find room for or that you can afford. Just be assured that healthy, quick, and delicious food can be prepared with the "basics."

A Healthy Exchanges Kitchen Equipment List

Good-quality nonstick skillets (medium, large)
Good-quality saucepans (small, medium, large)
Glass mixing bowls (small, medium, large)

Glass measures (1-cup, 2-cup, 4-cup, 8-cup)
Sharp knives (paring, chef, butcher)
Rubber spatulas

Wire whisks	4-inch round custard dishes
Measuring spoons	Glass pie plates
Measuring cups	8-by-8-inch glass baking dishes
Large mixing spoons	Cake pans (9-by-9-inch, 9-by-13-inch)
Egg separator	10¾-by-7-by-1½-inch biscuit pan
Covered jar	Cookie sheets (good nonstick ones)
Vegetable parer	Jelly-roll pan
Grater	Muffin tins
Potato masher	5-by-9-inch bread pan
Electric mixer	Plastic colander
Electric blender	Cutting board
Electric skillet	Pie wedge server
Cooking timer	Square-shaped server
Slow cooker	Can opener (I prefer manual)
Air popper for popcorn	Rolling pin

Kitchen scales (unless you *always* use my recipes)
Wire racks for cooling baked goods
Electric toaster oven (to conserve energy for those times when only one item is being baked or for a recipe that requires a short baking time)

How to Read a Healthy Exchanges Recipe

The Healthy Exchanges Nutritional Analysis

Before using these recipes, you may wish to consult your physician or health-care provider to be sure they are appropriate for you. The information in this book is not intended to take the place of any medical advice. It reflects my experiences, studies, research, and opinions regarding healthy eating.

Each recipe includes nutritional information calculated in three ways:

Healthy Exchanges Weight Loss Choices™ or Exchanges
Calories, fiber, and fat grams
Diabetic exchanges

In every Healthy Exchanges recipe, the diabetic exchanges have been calculated by a Registered Dietitian. All the other calculations were done by computer, using the Food Processor II software. When the ingredient listing gives more than one choice, the first ingredient listed is the one used in the recipe analysis. Due to inevitable variations in the ingredients you choose to use, the nutritional values should be considered approximate.

The annotation "(limited)" following Protein counts in some recipes indicates that consumption of whole eggs should be limited to four per week.

Please note the following symbols:

☆ This star means read the recipe's directions carefully for special instructions about **division** of ingredients.

✱ This symbol indicates **FREEZES WELL.**

A Few Cooking Terms to Ease the Way

Everyone can learn to cook the *Healthy Exchanges Way*. It's simple, it's quick, and the results are delicious! If you've tended to avoid the kitchen because you find recipe instructions confusing or complicated, I hope I can help you feel more confident. I'm not offering a full cooking course here, just some terms I use often that I know you'll want to understand.

Bake: To cook food in the oven; sometimes called roasting

Beat: To mix very fast with a spoon, wire whisk, or electric mixer

Blend: To mix two or more ingredients together thoroughly so that the mixture is smooth

Boil: To cook in liquid until bubbles form

Brown: To cook at low to medium-low heat until ingredients turn brown

Chop: To cut food into small pieces with a knife, blender, or food processor

Combine: To mix ingredients together with a spoon

Cool: To let stand at room temperature until food is no longer hot to the touch

Dice: To chop into small, even-sized pieces

Drain: To pour off liquid; sometimes you will need to reserve the liquid to use in the recipe, so please read carefully

Drizzle: To sprinkle drops of liquid (for example, chocolate syrup) lightly over the top of food

Fold in: To combine delicate ingredients with other foods by using a gentle, circular motion (for example, adding Cool Whip Lite to an already stirred-up bowl of pudding)

Preheat: To heat your oven to the desired temperature, usually about 10 minutes before you put your food in to bake

Sauté: To cook in a skillet or frying pan until the food is soft

Simmer: To cook in a small amount of liquid over low heat; this lets the flavors blend without too much liquid evaporating

Whisk: To beat with a wire whisk until mixture is well mixed; don't worry about finesse here, just use some elbow grease!

How to Measure

I try to make it as easy as possible by providing more than one measurement for many ingredients in my recipes—both the weight in ounces and the amount measured by a measuring cup, for example. Just remember:

- You measure **solids** (flour, Cool Whip Lite, yogurt, nonfat dry milk powder) in your set of separate measuring cups (¼, ⅓, ½, 1 cup)

- You measure **liquids** (Diet Mountain Dew, water, juice) in the clear glass or plastic measuring cups that measure ounces, cups, and pints. Set the cup on a level surface and pour the liquid into it, or you may get too much.

- You can use your measuring spoon set for liquids or solids. **Note:** Don't pour a liquid like an extract into a measuring spoon held over the bowl in case you overpour; instead, do it over the sink.

Here are a few handy equivalents:

3 teaspoons	equals	1 tablespoon
4 tablespoons	equals	¼ cup
5⅓ tablespoons	equals	⅓ cup
8 tablespoons	equals	½ cup
10⅔ tablespoons	equals	⅔ cup
12 tablespoons	equals	¾ cup
16 tablespoons	equals	1 cup
2 cups	equals	1 pint
4 cups	equals	1 quart
8 ounces liquid	equals	1 fluid cup

That's it. Now, ready, set, cook!

The Recipes

Magnificent

Muffins

I've always loved collecting old-fashioned kitchen utensils. Perhaps my favorite old-timey items are muffin tins—their intriguing and varied patterns pressed and pleated into the metal. If you've been looking for something to give your kitchen that cozy, country feel, why not start picking up old muffin tins at garage sales to hang on the walls?

Muffins are beloved by just about everyone for their charming, crusty appearance as much as for their scrumptious taste. They're also adored because they're easier to prepare than they look! I remember how surprised my kids were when their mom served up fresh blueberry muffins one Sunday morning some years ago. They knew I was working full-time and going to school at night, and they were thrilled I'd managed to squeeze some baking time in. (I never told them how fast I could stir up such muffin magic—I enjoyed their appreciation way too much!)

You can just imagine how much fun the staff at Healthy Exchanges had while I was testing the recipes for this book! Think of it—fresh muffins two, three, four times a day to nibble on. They seemed extra-motivated during those weeks, I remember.

There's a terrific variety of muffin choices in this section, and they are wonderfully simple to prepare and serve. If you're usually rushed in the morning (and who isn't?), get as much of the prep work done as you can before you go to bed so that you can spend whatever time you *do* have before work reading the paper and munching away!

Muffins aren't only for breakfast or brunch, of course. I think you'll be intrigued by my **Summer Garden Muffins**, which are more savory than sweet. And you'll enjoy the bounty of the garden—yours or the farmer's—when you stir up those **Rhubarb Patch Muffins**. If you really want to dazzle your kids, you couldn't do better than serve 'em **Zach's Breakfast Muffins!**

For the best possible result, fill unused muffin wells with water. It protects the muffin tin and ensures even baking.

Magnificent Muffins

Zach's Breakfast Muffins

It's every kid's favorite sandwich, and for most of us, the affection for "PB & J" never really goes away. I figured, why not a nutty-sweet muffin that celebrates that passion? ☻ Serves 8

⅔ *cup Carnation Nonfat Dry Milk Powder*
1 *cup water*
¼ *cup Peter Pan reduced-fat peanut butter*
1 *egg or equivalent in egg substitute*
¼ *cup pourable Sugar Twin*
1½ *cups Bisquick Reduced Fat Baking Mix*
2 *tablespoons spreadable fruit (any flavor)*

Preheat oven to 375 degrees. Spray 8 wells of a 12-hole muffin pan with butter-flavored cooking spray or line with paper liners. In a large bowl, combine dry milk powder and water. Stir in peanut butter, egg, and Sugar Twin. Add baking mix. Mix just until combined. Evenly spoon batter into prepared muffin wells. Top each with ¾ teaspoon spreadable fruit. Bake for 15 to 20 minutes or until a toothpick inserted in center comes out clean. Place muffin pan on a wire rack and let set for 5 minutes. Remove muffins from pan and continue cooling on wire rack.

Each serving equals:

HE: 1 Bread • ⅔ Protein • ½ Fat • ¼ Skim Milk • ¼ Fruit • 3 Optional Calories

---

169 Calories • 5 gm Fat • 6 gm Protein • 25 gm Carbohydrate • 338 mg Sodium • 90 mg Calcium • 1 gm Fiber

---

DIABETIC: 1½ Starch/Carbohydrate • ½ Meat • ½ Fat

Jumbo Lemon-Blueberry Muffins ❄

There are some combinations that taste as if they were joined in heaven, and this is definitely one of them. These are extra-big, extra-flavorful, and extra-ordinary—try them and see if you don't agree! These need to be baked in a muffin tin that makes LARGE muffins, so treat yourself to the perfect pan, and serve these often!

🌣 Serves 8

1½ cups all-purpose flour
1 (4-serving) package JELL-O sugar-free lemon gelatin
½ cup pourable Sugar Twin
1 teaspoon baking powder
½ teaspoon baking soda
1½ cups fresh blueberries
¼ cup (1 ounce) chopped walnuts

¾ cup Yoplait plain fat-free yogurt
⅓ cup Carnation Nonfat Dry Milk Powder
1 egg or equivalent in egg substitute
½ cup Diet Mountain Dew
1 teaspoon vanilla extract

Preheat oven to 400 degrees. Spray 8 wells of a 12-cup *large*-size muffin pan with butter-flavored cooking spray or line with paper liners. In a large bowl, combine flour, dry gelatin, Sugar Twin, baking powder, and baking soda. Stir in blueberries and walnuts. In a medium bowl, combine yogurt and dry milk powder. Add egg, Diet Mountain Dew, and vanilla extract. Mix well to combine. Add yogurt mixture to flour mixture. Mix gently just until combined. Evenly spoon batter into prepared muffin wells. Bake for 15 to 20 minutes or until a toothpick inserted in center comes out clean. Place muffin pan on a wire rack and let set for 5 minutes. Remove muffins from pan and continue cooling on wire rack.

Each serving equals:

HE: 1 Bread • ¼ Skim Milk • ¼ Protein • ¼ Fruit • ¼ Fat • 11 Optional Calories

155 Calories • 3 gm Fat • 6 gm Protein • 26 gm Carbohydrate • 208 mg Sodium • 122 mg Calcium • 2 gm Fiber

DIABETIC: 1½ Starch/Carbohydrate • ½ Fat

Morning Glory Muffins

How can any day be less than glorious when you've got these moist and scrumptious ways to greet the dawn? Even if you've got no fresh fruit in the house, that bag of apricots in your cabinet means muffins for breakfast! ❂ Serves 8

> 1 cup self-rising flour
> 3 tablespoons pourable Sugar Twin
> ½ cup skim milk
> 2 tablespoons Kraft fat-free mayonnaise
> 1 teaspoon vanilla extract
> ⅔ cup (3 ounces) chopped dried apricots

Preheat oven to 425 degrees. Spray 8 wells of a 12-hole muffin pan with butter-flavored cooking spray or line with paper liners. In a large bowl, combine flour and Sugar Twin. Add skim milk, mayonnaise, and vanilla extract. Mix well to combine. Fold in apricots. Fill prepared muffin wells ½ full. Bake for 10 to 12 minutes or until a toothpick inserted in center comes out clean. Lightly spray top of muffins with butter-flavored cooking spray. Place muffin pan on a wire rack and let set for 5 minutes. Remove muffins from pan and continue cooling on wire rack.

HINT: If you don't have self-rising flour, use 1 cup regular all-purpose flour, ½ teaspoon salt, and 1½ teaspoons baking powder.

Each serving equals:

> HE: ⅔ Bread • ½ Fruit • 10 Optional Calories
>
> ---
>
> 88 Calories • 0 gm Fat • 3 gm Protein •
> 19 gm Carbohydrate • 42 mg Sodium •
> 26 mg Calcium • 2 gm Fiber
>
> ---
>
> DIABETIC: ½ Starch • ½ Fruit

Breakfast Banana Muffins

If you've always loved banana bread and could nibble on a piece morning, noon, or night, then these will surely make you "rise and shine" without a single complaint! Besides tasting just great only minutes out of the oven, these are wonderful when frozen and reheated.   ☻   Serves 8

1½ cups all-purpose flour
2 tablespoons pourable
    Sugar Twin
1 (4-serving) package JELL-O
    sugar-free instant
    vanilla pudding mix
1 teaspoon baking powder
½ teaspoon baking soda
1 teaspoon ground cinnamon

¼ cup (1 ounce) chopped
    walnuts
⅔ cup (2 ripe medium)
    mashed bananas
1 cup unsweetened
    applesauce
1 egg or equivalent in egg
    substitute
1 teaspoon vanilla extract

Preheat oven to 375 degrees. Spray 8 wells of a 12-hole muffin pan with butter-flavored cooking spray or line with paper liners. In a large bowl, combine flour, Sugar Twin, dry pudding mix, baking powder, baking soda, cinnamon, and walnuts. In a small bowl, combine bananas, applesauce, egg, and vanilla extract. Add banana mixture to flour mixture. Mix gently just to combine. Evenly spoon batter into prepared muffin wells. Bake for 15 to 20 minutes or until a toothpick inserted in center comes out clean. Place muffin pan on a wire rack and let set for 5 minutes. Remove muffins from pan and continue cooling on wire rack.

Each serving equals:

HE: 1 Bread • ¾ Fruit • ¼ Protein • ¼ Fat •
13 Optional Calories

---

155 Calories • 3 gm Fat • 4 gm Protein •
28 gm Carbohydrate • 387 mg Sodium •
49 mg Calcium • 2 gm Fiber

DIABETIC: 1 Starch • 1 Fruit • ½ Fat

Banana-Graham Muffins

Love bananas? Love graham crackers? Then this recipe has your name on it! These nutty, fruity delights are a super way to treat your family to something special that doesn't take a lot of time to prepare. ☯ Serves 8

> ¾ cup purchased graham cracker crumbs or 12 (2½-inch)
> graham cracker squares, made into crumbs
> ¾ cup all-purpose flour
> 2 tablespoons Brown Sugar Twin
> 1½ teaspoons baking powder
> ½ teaspoon baking soda
> ¼ cup (1 ounce) chopped pecans
> ⅔ cup Carnation Nonfat Dry Milk Powder
> ½ cup water
> ⅓ cup Yoplait plain fat-free yogurt
> ¼ cup Kraft fat-free mayonnaise
> ⅔ cup (2 ripe medium) mashed bananas
> 1 teaspoon vanilla extract

Preheat oven to 375 degrees. Spray 8 wells of a 12-hole muffin pan with butter-flavored cooking spray or line with paper liners. In a large bowl, combine graham cracker crumbs, flour, Brown Sugar Twin, baking powder, baking soda, and pecans. In a medium bowl, combine dry milk powder and water. Stir in yogurt, mayonnaise, bananas, and vanilla extract. Add milk mixture to flour mixture. Mix just until combined. Evenly spoon batter into prepared muffin wells. Bake for 20 to 25 minutes or until a toothpick inserted in center comes out clean. Place muffin pan on a wire rack and let set for 5 minutes. Remove muffins from pan and continue cooling on wire rack.

HINT: A self-seal sandwich bag works great for crushing graham crackers.

Each serving equals:

HE: 1 Bread • ½ Fruit • ½ Fat • ¼ Skim Milk •
10 Optional Calories

---

151 Calories • 3 gm Fat • 5 gm Protein •
26 gm Carbohydrate • 341 mg Sodium •
145 mg Calcium • 1 gm Fiber

DIABETIC: 1 Starch • ½ Fruit • ½ Fat

Praline-Banana Muffins

I'm often teased about being the "Pecan Queen," but really, did the good Lord make a better nut than those beautiful bites? Pralines are one of New Orleans's claims to fame, but they're also high-sugar, high-fat pleasures best saved for very special occasions. For the rest of the year, why not get the flavor you crave in a healthy muffin?

● Serves 8

2 tablespoons Brown Sugar
    Twin
1 tablespoon Land O Lakes
    no-fat sour cream
2 tablespoons (½ ounce)
    chopped pecans
⅔ cup (2 ripe medium)
    mashed bananas
1 egg or equivalent in egg
    substitute

⅓ cup pourable Sugar Twin
⅔ cup unsweetened applesauce
1½ cups Aunt Jemima Lite
    Pancake Mix
1 (4-serving) package
    JELL-O sugar-free instant
    vanilla pudding mix

Preheat oven to 375 degrees. Spray 8 wells of a 12-hole muffin pan with butter-flavored cooking spray or line with paper liners. In a small bowl, combine Brown Sugar Twin and sour cream. Stir in pecans. Set aside. In a large bowl, combine bananas, egg, Sugar Twin, and applesauce. Add pancake mix and dry pudding. Mix just until combined. Evenly spoon batter into prepared muffin wells. Drop about 1 teaspoon pecan mixture on top of each muffin. Bake for 25 to 30 minutes or until a toothpick inserted in center comes out clean. Place muffin pan on a wire rack and let set for 5 minutes. Remove muffins from pan and continue cooling on wire rack.

Each serving equals:

HE: 1 Bread • ⅔ Fruit • ¼ Fat • ¼ Slider •
7 Optional Calories

151 Calories • 3 gm Fat • 5 gm Protein •
26 gm Carbohydrate • 466 mg Sodium •
143 mg Calcium • 3 gm Fiber

DIABETIC: 1 Starch • 1 Fruit

Banana-Strawberry Muffins

The swirl of spreadable fruit topping makes these muffins as pretty as anything I've ever served my family! And don't forget, the best kind of bananas for baking are the ones that are sweet, soft, and super-ripe. This is a really moist, heavy muffin—*mmm!*

Serves 8

> ¾ cup Yoplait plain fat-free yogurt
> ⅓ cup Carnation Nonfat Dry Milk Powder
> ¼ cup water
> 2 teaspoons white vinegar
> 1½ cups all-purpose flour
> 1 (4-serving) package JELL-O sugar-free instant vanilla pudding mix
> ½ cup pourable Sugar Twin
> 1½ teaspoons baking powder
> ½ teaspoon baking soda
> ⅔ cup (2 ripe medium) mashed bananas
> 2 tablespoons strawberry spreadable fruit

Preheat oven to 400 degrees. Spray 8 wells of a 12-hole muffin pan with butter-flavored cooking spray or line with paper liners. In a medium bowl, combine yogurt, dry milk powder, water, and vinegar. Set aside. In a large bowl, combine flour, dry pudding mix, Sugar Twin, baking powder, and baking soda. Add yogurt mixture and bananas to flour mixture. Mix well to combine. Spoon about 2 tablespoons batter into each prepared muffin well. Spoon about ¾ teaspoon spreadable fruit over top of each. Evenly top each with remaining batter. Using tines of a fork, gently swirl batter with spreadable fruit. Bake for 25 to 30 minutes. Place muffin pan on a wire rack and let set for 5 minutes. Remove muffins from pan and continue cooling on wire rack.

Each serving equals:

HE: 1 Bread • ¾ Fruit • ¼ Skim Milk •
18 Optional Calories

136 Calories • 0 gm Fat • 5 gm Protein •
29 gm Carbohydrate • 367 mg Sodium •
132 mg Calcium • 1 gm Fiber

DIABETIC: 1 Starch • 1 Fruit

Cranberry-Banana Muffins

In texture and flavor, cranberries and bananas make an intriguing partnership. The berries are colorful and tart, the bananas pale, soft, and sweet. Blended together in one terrific muffin, they double your pleasure in every bite! ☺ Serves 8

1½ cups all-purpose flour
1 (4-serving) package sugar-free instant banana cream pudding mix
¼ cup pourable Sugar Twin
1 teaspoon baking powder
½ teaspoon baking soda
½ teaspoon apple pie spice
1 cup chopped fresh or frozen cranberries
⅔ cup (2 ripe medium) mashed bananas
1 teaspoon vanilla extract
2 eggs or equivalent in egg substitute
½ cup unsweetened applesauce

Preheat oven to 375 degrees. Spray 8 wells of a 12-hole muffin pan with butter-flavored cooking spray or line with paper liners. In a large bowl, combine flour, dry pudding mix, Sugar Twin, baking powder, baking soda, and apple pie spice. Add cranberries. Mix well to combine. In a small bowl, combine bananas, vanilla extract, eggs, and applesauce. Add banana mixture to flour mixture. Mix just until combined. Evenly spoon batter into prepared muffin wells. Bake for 22 to 27 minutes or until a toothpick inserted in center comes out clean. Place muffin pan on a wire rack and let set for 5 minutes. Remove muffins from pan and continue cooling on wire rack.

Each serving equals:

HE: 1 Bread • ¾ Fruit • ¼ Protein (limited) • 16 Optional Calories

142 Calories • 2 gm Fat • 4 gm Protein • 27 gm Carbohydrate • 326 mg Sodium • 45 mg Calcium • 2 gm Fiber

DIABETIC: 1 Starch • 1 Fruit

Mini Raisin-Banana Muffins

Kids just love mini-muffins, and I've yet to meet an adult who doesn't smile at the sight of a plate heaped high with these tiny treats! It's hard to feel deprived when you get to enjoy three of these splendid mouth-fuls. ☻ Serves 12 (3 each)

1½ cups all-purpose flour

¼ cup (¾ ounce) quick oats

1 (4-serving) package JELL-O sugar-free instant vanilla pudding mix

1 teaspoon baking soda

1 teaspoon apple pie spice

⅓ cup pourable Sugar Twin

1 cup unsweetened applesauce

1 egg, beaten, or equivalent in egg substitute

1 cup (3 ripe medium) mashed bananas

½ cup raisins

¼ cup (1 ounce) chopped pecans

Preheat oven to 350 degrees. Spray three 12-hole mini muffin pans with butter-flavored cooking spray. In a large bowl, combine flour, oats, dry pudding mix, baking soda, apple pie spice, and Sugar Twin. In a small bowl, combine applesauce, egg, and bananas. Add applesauce mixture to flour mixture. Mix well to combine. Stir in raisins and pecans. Evenly spoon mixture into prepared muffin wells. Bake for 12 to 15 minutes. Place muffin pans on wire racks and let set for 5 minutes. Remove muffins from pans and continue cooling on wire racks.

Each serving equals:

HE: 1 Fruit • ¾ Bread • ¼ Fat • 16 Optional Calories

130 Calories • 2 gm Fat • 3 gm Protein •
25 gm Carbohydrate • 222 mg Sodium •
10 mg Calcium • 2 gm Fiber

DIABETIC: 1 Fruit • 1 Starch • ½ Fat

Double Chocolate–
Banana Muffins

Talk about truly luscious, and you're probably talking about these rich and creamy good-enough-to-be-dessert muffins! Layering flavors, as I do here with the two kinds of chocolate, makes a kind of culinary magic sure to make you smile. ☻ Serves 8

1½ cups all-purpose flour
¾ cup pourable Sugar Twin
¼ cup unsweetened cocoa
1 teaspoon baking powder
½ teaspoon baking soda
1⅓ cups (4 ripe medium) mashed bananas

1 egg or equivalent in egg substitute
2 tablespoons vegetable oil
¼ cup Land O Lakes no-fat sour cream
¼ cup (1 ounce) mini chocolate chips

Preheat oven to 375 degrees. Spray 8 wells of a 12-hole muffin pan with butter-flavored cooking spray or line with paper liners. In a large bowl, combine flour, Sugar Twin, cocoa, baking powder, and baking soda. In a small bowl, combine bananas, egg, vegetable oil, and sour cream. Add banana mixture to flour mixture. Mix gently to combine. Fold in chocolate chips. Evenly spoon batter into prepared muffin wells. Bake for 20 to 25 minutes or until a toothpick inserted in center comes out clean. Place muffin pan on a wire rack and let set for 5 minutes. Remove muffins from pan and continue cooling on wire rack.

Each serving equals:

HE: 1 Bread • 1 Fruit • ¾ Fat • ½ Slider • 10 Optional Calories

186 Calories • 6 gm Fat • 4 gm Protein • 29 gm Carbohydrate • 159 mg Sodium • 54 mg Calcium • 2 gm Fiber

DIABETIC: 1 Starch • 1 Fruit • 1 Fat

Strawberry Morning Muffins

I get up very, very early most mornings, way before the sun is fully up. What gets me going, besides my enthusiasm for the work I do with Healthy Exchanges, is something fresh and sweet from the oven. If it's got strawberries in it, then I'm raring to go moments later!   ☻   Serves 8

1½ cups all-purpose flour
1 (4-serving) package JELL-O
    sugar-free instant
    vanilla pudding mix
¼ cup pourable Sugar Twin
1 teaspoon baking powder
½ teaspoon baking soda
1 cup finely chopped fresh
    strawberries

¼ cup (1 ounce) chopped
    walnuts
½ cup unsweetened applesauce
1 teaspoon vanilla extract
1 egg or equivalent in egg
    substitute
⅓ cup skim milk

Preheat oven to 375 degrees. Spray 8 wells of a 12-hole muffin pan with butter-flavored cooking spray or line with paper liners. In a large bowl, combine flour, dry pudding mix, Sugar Twin, baking powder, and baking soda. Stir in strawberries and walnuts. In a small bowl, combine applesauce, vanilla extract, egg, and skim milk. Add applesauce mixture to flour mixture. Mix just until combined. Evenly spoon batter into prepared muffin wells. Bake for 20 to 25 minutes or until a toothpick inserted in center comes out clean. Place muffin pan on a wire rack and let set for 5 minutes. Remove muffins from pan and continue cooling on wire rack.

Each serving equals:

HE: 1 Bread • ¼ Protein • ¼ Fruit • ¼ Fat •
19 Optional Calories

143 Calories • 3 gm Fat • 4 gm Protein •
25 gm Carbohydrate • 319 mg Sodium •
59 mg Calcium • 1 gm Fiber

DIABETIC: 2 Starch

Rhubarb Patch Muffins

If your only experience with rhubarb is with the frozen kind, I urge you to investigate fresh rhubarb this year. It's such a beautiful color, it even smells good while you're chopping it up, and it's full of good-for-you vitamins. These festive muffins are terrific for a late-spring brunch. ●   Serves 8

1½ cups all-purpose flour

1 teaspoon baking powder

½ teaspoon baking soda

1 (4-serving) package JELL-O sugar-free instant vanilla pudding mix

¼ cup Brown Sugar Twin

1 cup finely diced rhubarb

¼ cup (1 ounce) chopped walnuts

1 cup unsweetened applesauce

1 egg or equivalent in egg substitute

1 teaspoon vanilla extract

¼ cup skim milk

1 tablespoon pourable Sugar Twin

¼ teaspoon ground cinnamon

Preheat oven to 375 degrees. Spray 8 wells of a 12-hole muffin pan with butter-flavored cooking spray or line with paper liners. In a large bowl, combine flour, baking powder, baking soda, dry pudding mix, and Brown Sugar Twin. Stir in rhubarb and walnuts. In a small bowl, combine applesauce, egg, vanilla extract, and skim milk. Add applesauce mixture to flour mixture. Mix just until combined. Evenly spoon batter into prepared muffin wells. In a small bowl, combine Sugar Twin and cinnamon. Sprinkle cinnamon mixture evenly over top of muffins. Bake for 22 to 27 minutes or until a toothpick inserted in center comes out clean. Place muffin pan on a wire rack and let set for 5 minutes. Remove muffins from pan and continue cooling on wire rack.

Each serving equals:

HE: 1 Bread • ¼ Protein • ¼ Fruit • ¼ Fat • ¼ Vegetable • 19 Optional Calories

147 Calories • 3 gm Fat • 4 gm Protein • 26 gm Carbohydrate • 319 mg Sodium • 68 mg Calcium • 2 gm Fiber

DIABETIC: 2 Starch

Spring Medley Muffins

I love it when tiny green shoots of young plants start peeking up through the ground. When I see them, I know that winter is on its way out—and rebirth is in the air! Why not give yourself the same fresh start the season provides, by choosing to eat a good breakfast every morning—and starting with these flavorful muffins?

❍ Serves 8 (2 muffins each)

⅔ cup Carnation Nonfat
  Dry Milk Powder

1 cup water

2 teaspoons white vinegar

1½ cups all-purpose flour

½ cup pourable Sugar Twin

1 teaspoon baking powder

½ teaspoon baking soda

¼ cup (1 ounce) chopped
  walnuts

1 cup finely diced rhubarb

1 cup diced fresh strawberries

2 tablespoons raisins

1 egg or equivalent in egg
  substitute

Preheat oven to 400 degrees. Spray 16 wells in muffin pans with butter-flavored cooking spray or line with paper liners. In a small bowl, combine dry milk powder, water, and vinegar. Set aside. In a large bowl, combine flour, Sugar Twin, baking powder, baking soda, and walnuts. Gently stir in rhubarb, strawberries, and raisins. Stir egg into milk mixture. Add milk mixture to flour mixture. Mix just until combined. Fill prepared muffin wells ½ full. Bake for 20 to 25 minutes or until a toothpick inserted in center comes out clean. Place muffin pans on a wire rack and let set for 5 minutes. Remove muffins from pan and continue cooling on wire rack.

Each serving equals:

HE: 1 Bread • ¼ Skim Milk • ¼ Protein • ¼ Fruit • ¼ Fat • ¼ Vegetable • 6 Optional Calories

151 Calories • 3 gm Fat • 6 gm Protein • 25 gm Carbohydrate • 180 mg Sodium • 129 mg Calcium • 2 gm Fiber

DIABETIC: 1 Starch • ½ Fruit • ½ Fat

Blueberry Horizon Muffins

I have always liked the word "horizon" because it makes me think about all the good things around the bend, just out of sight. Why not think of your healthy lifestyle as your commitment to what's beyond the horizon, and nourish yourself really well with these wonderfully fruity delights?   ☺   Serves 8

⅓ cup (2 ounces) quick oats
½ cup unsweetened orange juice
⅓ cup unsweetened applesauce
1 egg or equivalent in egg substitute
⅓ cup + 2 tablespoons pourable Sugar Twin ☆

1 cup all-purpose flour
1 teaspoon baking powder
½ teaspoon baking soda
¾ cup fresh blueberries
¼ cup (1 ounce) chopped walnuts
½ teaspoon ground cinnamon

Preheat oven to 375 degrees. Spray 8 wells of a 12-hole muffin pan with butter-flavored cooking spray or line with paper liners. In a large bowl, combine oats and orange juice. Stir in applesauce and egg. Add ⅓ cup Sugar Twin, flour, baking powder, and baking soda. Mix just until combined. Fold in blueberries and walnuts. Evenly spoon batter into prepared muffin wells. In a small bowl, combine remaining 2 tablespoons Sugar Twin and cinnamon. Sprinkle about ¾ teaspoon cinnamon mixture over top of each muffin. Bake for 18 to 22 minutes or until a toothpick inserted in center comes out clean. Place muffin pan on a wire rack and let set for 5 minutes. Remove muffins from pan and continue cooling on wire rack.

Each serving equals:

HE: 1 Bread • ⅓ Fruit • ¼ Protein • ¼ Fat • 5 Optional Calories

119 Calories • 3 gm Fat • 3 gm Protein • 20 gm Carbohydrate • 150 mg Sodium • 48 mg Calcium • 2 gm Fiber

DIABETIC: 1 Starch/Carbohydrate • ½ Fat

Cranberry-Orange Muffins

This is an especially flavorful combination of fruits, with the juicy orange sweetness combining beautifully with the tart red cranberries. And wait until you taste the creamy miracle that no-fat sour cream provides in this easy recipe! ● Serves 8

1 cup Land O Lakes no-fat
    sour cream
¼ cup unsweetened orange
    juice
1 egg or equivalent in egg
    substitute
½ cup pourable Sugar Twin
2 tablespoons Brown Sugar
    Twin

¼ cup reduced-calorie
    margarine, melted
1½ cups all-purpose flour
2 teaspoons baking powder
1 teaspoon baking soda
1 teaspoon ground cinnamon
1½ cups chopped fresh or
    frozen cranberries

Preheat oven to 375 degrees. Spray 8 wells of a 12-hole muffin pan with butter-flavored cooking spray or line with paper liners. In a small bowl, combine sour cream, orange juice, egg, Sugar Twin, Brown Sugar Twin, and margarine. In a large bowl, combine flour, baking powder, baking soda, and cinnamon. Add sour cream mixture to flour mixture. Mix just until combined. Stir in cranberries. Evenly spoon batter into prepared muffin wells. Bake for 25 to 30 minutes or until muffins are golden brown and a toothpick inserted in center comes out clean. Place muffin pan on a wire rack and let set for 5 minutes. Remove muffins from pan and continue cooling on wire rack.

Each serving equals:

HE: 1 Bread • ¾ Fat • ¼ Fruit • ¼ Slider •
17 Optional Calories

147 Calories • 3 gm Fat • 4 gm Protein •
26 gm Carbohydrate • 356 mg Sodium •
111 mg Calcium • 2 gm Fiber

DIABETIC: 1½ Starch/Carbohydrate • 1 Fat

Georgia Peach Muffins

So many people (including my daughter, Becky) consider peaches the most luscious fruit available, whether enjoyed fresh-picked and ripe, or handy in the pantry from a can. These Southern-style muffins are as "peachy-keen" as I could make them!   ☻   Serves 8

2 cups (one 16-ounce can)
    sliced peaches, packed
    in fruit juice, drained,
    and ½ cup liquid
    reserved
1½ cups all-purpose flour
¼ cup pourable Sugar Twin
1 teaspoon baking powder
1 teaspoon baking soda

2 tablespoons (½ ounce)
    chopped pecans
⅓ cup Yoplait plain fat-free
    yogurt
2 tablespoons Kraft fat-free
    mayonnaise
1 teaspoon vanilla extract
2 tablespoons peach spreadable
    fruit

Preheat oven to 400 degrees. Spray 8 wells of a 12-hole muffin pan with butter-flavored cooking spray or line with paper liners. Finely chop peaches. In a large bowl, combine flour, Sugar Twin, baking powder, baking soda, and pecans. Stir in chopped peaches. In a medium bowl, combine yogurt, mayonnaise, vanilla extract, reserved peach liquid, and spreadable fruit. Add yogurt mixture to flour mixture. Mix gently to combine. Evenly spoon batter into prepared muffin wells. Bake for 16 to 22 minutes or until a toothpick inserted in center comes out clean. Place muffin pan on a wire rack and let set for 5 minutes. Remove muffins from pan and continue cooling on wire rack.

Each serving equals:

HE: 1 Bread • ¾ Fruit • ¼ Fat • 9 Optional Calories

137 Calories • 1 gm Fat • 3 gm Protein •
29 gm Carbohydrate • 261 mg Sodium •
60 mg Calcium • 2 gm Fiber

DIABETIC: 1 Starch • 1 Fruit

Rise-and-Shine Apple Muffins

I remember a song the kids used to sing that asked everyone to "rise and shine and give God your glory, glory!" It's a wonderful feeling to rededicate yourself each new day to your faith and to the people you love. You can show your caring with these high-spirited muffins.   ◐   Serves 6

1 cup + 2 tablespoons
    Bisquick Reduced Fat
    Baking Mix
2 tablespoons pourable
    Sugar Twin
1 tablespoon Brown Sugar
    Twin
1 teaspoon apple pie spice
6 tablespoons raisins

¼ cup (1 ounce) chopped
    walnuts
½ cup unsweetened applesauce
¼ cup skim milk
1 egg or equivalent in egg
    substitute
1 cup (2 small) cored, peeled,
    and finely chopped
    cooking apples

Preheat oven to 400 degrees. Spray the wells of a 6-hole muffin pan with butter-flavored cooking spray or line with paper liners. In a large bowl, combine baking mix, Sugar Twin, Brown Sugar Twin, and apple pie spice. Add raisins and walnuts. Mix well to combine. In a small bowl, combine applesauce, skim milk, and egg. Add applesauce mixture to baking mix mixture. Mix just until combined. Stir in apples. Spoon a scant ⅔ cup batter into each prepared muffin well. Bake for 15 to 20 minutes or until a toothpick inserted in center comes out clean. Place muffin pan on a wire rack and let set for 5 minutes. Remove muffins from pan and continue cooling on wire rack.

Each serving equals:

HE: 1 Bread • 1 Fruit • ⅓ Protein • ⅓ Fat •
7 Optional Calories

177 Calories • 5 gm Fat • 4 gm Protein •
29 gm Carbohydrate • 279 mg Sodium •
46 mg Calcium • 1 gm Fiber

DIABETIC: 1 Starch • 1 Fruit • ½ Fat

Maple Applesauce Muffins

You open the cabinet and spot your bottle of healthy maple syrup. *Mmm,* you think, but you aren't in the mood for pancakes this morning. Grab the bottle anyway, and stir up this easy blend of nuts and apple flavor. What a tasty way to start the day! ☻   Serves 8

> 1½ cups all-purpose flour
> 2 teaspoons baking powder
> 2 tablespoons Brown Sugar Twin
> 1 (4-serving) package JELL-O sugar-free instant vanilla pudding mix
> ¼ cup (1 ounce) chopped walnuts
> ¾ cup raisins
> 1 cup unsweetened applesauce
> 1 egg or equivalent in egg substitute
> ⅓ cup Cary's Sugar Free Maple Syrup

Preheat oven to 375 degrees. Spray 8 wells of a 12-hole muffin pan with butter-flavored cooking spray or line with paper liners. In a large bowl, combine flour, baking powder, Brown Sugar Twin, and dry pudding mix. Stir in walnuts and raisins. In a small bowl, combine applesauce, egg, and maple syrup. Add applesauce mixture to flour mixture. Mix just until combined. Evenly spoon batter into prepared muffin wells. Bake for 20 to 25 minutes or until a toothpick inserted in center comes out clean. Place muffin pan on a wire rack and let set for 5 minutes. Remove muffins from pan and continue cooling on wire rack.

Each serving equals:

HE: 1 Bread • 1 Fruit • ¼ Protein • ¼ Fat •
¼ Slider • 1 Optional Calorie

191 Calories • 3 gm Fat • 4 gm Protein •
37 gm Carbohydrate • 320 mg Sodium •
85 mg Calcium • 2 gm Fiber

DIABETIC: 1½ Starch • 1 Fruit

Carrot-Pineapple Muffins

Bet you're not used to including vegetables in your breakfast menu very often, but that's about to change! Grating carrots may seem like too much work for the morning, so you might choose to do this task the night before and seal the carrots in a plastic bag. The flavor of these splendid treats will convince you the extra work was worth it! ☻ Serves 8

> 1½ cups all-purpose flour
> 1 (4-serving) package
>   JELL-O sugar-free instant vanilla pudding mix
> 1 teaspoon baking powder
> ½ teaspoon baking soda
> 1 teaspoon apple pie spice
> 1 cup grated carrots
> ¼ cup (1 ounce) chopped walnuts
> ⅓ cup unsweetened applesauce
> 1 egg or equivalent in egg substitute
> 1 cup (one 8-ounce can) crushed pineapple, packed in fruit juice,
>   undrained
> 1 teaspoon vanilla extract

Preheat oven to 375 degrees. Spray 8 wells of a 12-hole muffin pan with butter-flavored cooking spray. In a large bowl, combine flour, dry pudding mix, baking powder, baking soda, and apple pie spice. Stir in carrots and walnuts. In a small bowl, combine applesauce, egg, undrained pineapple, and vanilla extract. Add applesauce mixture to flour mixture. Mix well to combine. Evenly spoon batter into prepared muffin wells. Bake for 30 to 35 minutes or until a toothpick inserted in center comes out clean. Place muffin pan on a wire rack and let set for 5 minutes. Remove muffins from pan and continue cooling on wire rack.

Each serving equals:

HE: 1 Bread • ⅓ Fruit • ¼ Protein • ¼ Fat •
¼ Vegetable • 13 Optional Calories

---

159 Calories • 3 gm Fat • 4 gm Protein •
29 gm Carbohydrate • 319 mg Sodium •
52 mg Calcium • 2 gm Fiber

DIABETIC: 1½ Starch/Carbohydrate • ½ Fat

Apricot-Walnut Muffins

Each of these muffins delivers a nice wallop of fiber, which medical research indicates is especially good for your heart! The oats provide a mouth-pleasing texture (as do the nuts and bits of fruit), so you'll be satisfying your taste buds as well as your soul.

◐ Serves 8

> ½ cup (1½ ounces) quick oats
>
> 1 cup + 2 tablespoons Bisquick Reduced Fat Baking Mix
>
> ½ cup pourable Sugar Twin
>
> 1 teaspoon baking powder
>
> ⅔ cup (3 ounces) chopped dried apricots
>
> ¼ cup (1 ounce) chopped walnuts
>
> ½ cup skim milk
>
> 1 egg, well beaten, or equivalent in egg substitute
>
> 1 teaspoon vanilla extract

Preheat oven to 375 degrees. Spray 8 wells of a 12-hole muffin pan with butter-flavored cooking spray. In a large bowl, combine oats, baking mix, Sugar Twin, baking powder, apricots, and walnuts. In a small bowl, combine skim milk, egg, and vanilla extract. Add milk mixture to baking mix mixture. Mix well to combine. Evenly spoon batter into prepared muffin wells. Bake for 20 to 25 minutes or until a toothpick inserted in center comes out clean. Place muffin pan on a wire rack and let set for 5 minutes. Remove muffins from pan and continue cooling on wire rack.

Each serving equals:

> HE: 1 Bread • ½ Fruit • ¼ Protein • ¼ Fat •
> 12 Optional Calories
>
> ---
> 144 Calories • 4 gm Fat • 4 gm Protein •
> 23 gm Carbohydrate • 275 mg Sodium •
> 80 mg Calcium • 2 gm Fiber
>
> ---
> DIABETIC: 1 Starch • ½ Fruit • ½ Fat

Pineapple-Walnut Spice Muffins

The scrumptious aroma coming from the oven when these are baking is enough to bring family members running to the kitchen! The apple pie spice makes these wildly fruity muffins even more delectable. (And because my grandsons, Zach and Josh, love these, they don't even have to ask—I just stock up on pineapple when they're coming for a visit!) ☻ Serves 8

1½ cups all-purpose flour
½ cup pourable Sugar Twin
¼ cup (1 ounce) chopped walnuts
1 teaspoon baking powder
½ teaspoon baking soda
1 teaspoon apple pie spice
½ cup unsweetened applesauce

1 egg or equivalent in egg substitute
1 cup (one 8-ounce can) crushed pineapple, packed in fruit juice, undrained
1 teaspoon coconut extract
1 tablespoon + 1 teaspoon flaked coconut

Preheat oven to 400 degrees. Spray 8 wells of a 12-hole muffin pan with butter-flavored cooking spray or line with paper liners. In a large bowl, combine flour, Sugar Twin, walnuts, baking powder, baking soda, and apple pie spice. In a small bowl, combine applesauce, egg, undrained pineapple, and coconut extract. Add applesauce mixture to flour mixture. Mix just until combined. Fill prepared muffin wells ¾ full. Sprinkle ½ teaspoon coconut over top of each. Bake for 15 to 20 minutes or until a toothpick inserted in center comes out clean. Place muffin pan on a wire rack and let set for 5 minutes. Remove muffins from pan and continue cooling on wire rack.

Each serving equals:

HE: 1 Bread • ⅓ Fruit • ¼ Protein • ¼ Fat • 12 Optional Calories

147 Calories • 3 gm Fat • 4 gm Protein • 26 gm Carbohydrate • 151 mg Sodium • 49 mg Calcium • 1 gm Fiber

DIABETIC: 1 Starch • ½ Fruit • ½ Fat

Pumpkin Harvest Muffins

Canned pumpkin, available all year long at the supermarket, gives these taste treats a truly lovely color as well as great flavor! Because these muffins are so moist, the raisins "blossom" beautifully as they bake and turn out wonderfully plump.　❂　Serves 8

1½ cups all-purpose flour
⅓ cup pourable Sugar Twin
⅔ cup Carnation Nonfat Dry Milk Powder
2 teaspoons baking soda
2 teaspoons pumpkin pie spice
¼ cup Brown Sugar Twin
½ cup raisins
2 cups (one 15-ounce can) pumpkin
2 eggs or equivalent in egg substitute
2 teaspoons vanilla extract

Preheat oven to 375 degrees. Spray 8 wells of a 12-hole muffin pan with butter-flavored cooking spray or line with paper liners. In a large bowl, combine flour, Sugar Twin, dry milk powder, baking soda, pumpkin pie spice, Brown Sugar Twin, and raisins. In a small bowl, combine pumpkin, eggs, and vanilla extract. Add pumpkin mixture to flour mixture. Mix just until combined. Evenly spoon batter into prepared muffin wells. Bake for 20 to 30 minutes or until a toothpick inserted in center comes out clean. Place muffin pan on a wire rack and let set for 5 minutes. Remove muffins from pan and continue cooling on wire rack.

Each serving equals:

HE: 1 Bread • ½ Fruit • ½ Vegetable • ¼ Skim Milk • ¼ Protein (limited) • 5 Optional Calories

169 Calories • 1 gm Fat • 7 gm Protein • 33 gm Carbohydrate • 366 mg Sodium • 99 mg Calcium • 3 gm Fiber

DIABETIC: 1½ Starch/Carbohydrate • ½ Fruit

Cornbread Muffins

Cornbread has a unique flavor that really complements spicy food, so if you're planning a lively breakfast entree or even just spooning some salsa on your eggs, these corn-y muffins will add just the right touch! Now that my son Tommy and daughter-in-law Angie have settled in the Southwest, we're trying that region's recipes more than ever! ☻ Serves 12

1 cup Carnation Nonfat Dry
    Milk Powder
1 cup water
2 teaspoons white vinegar
1 cup (6 ounces) yellow
    cornmeal
3/4 cup all-purpose flour
1 1/2 teaspoons baking powder

1/2 teaspoon baking soda
1/4 cup pourable Sugar Twin
1/4 cup reduced-calorie
    margarine
1 egg, slightly beaten, or
    equivalent in egg
    substitute

Preheat oven to 375 degrees. Spray a 12-hole muffin pan with butter-flavored cooking spray or line with paper liners. In a small bowl, combine dry milk powder, water, and vinegar. Set aside. In a large bowl, combine cornmeal, flour, baking powder, baking soda, and Sugar Twin. Stir margarine and egg into milk mixture. Add milk mixture to cornmeal mixture. Mix just until combined. Fill prepared muffin wells about 2/3 full. Bake for 15 to 20 minutes or until lightly browned. Place muffin pan on a wire rack and let set for 5 minutes. Remove muffins from pan and eat warm or continue cooling on wire rack.

Each serving equals:

HE: 1 Bread • 1/2 Fat • 1/4 Skim Milk •
7 Optional Calories

106 Calories • 2 gm Fat • 4 gm Protein •
18 gm Carbohydrate • 169 mg Sodium •
107 mg Calcium • 1 gm Fiber

DIABETIC: 1 Starch • 1/2 Fat

Swiss Cheese and Dill Muffins

No time for breakfast as you race out the door to your job, your classes, or your child's baseball practice? No problem! These tangy muffins are amazingly filling, delightfully hearty, and ready to toss in a brown bag and bring along.   ◐   Serves 8

1½ cups Bisquick Reduced Fat Baking Mix
5 (¾-ounce) slices Kraft reduced-fat Swiss cheese, shredded
2 teaspoons pourable Sugar Twin
⅔ cup skim milk
1 egg or equivalent in egg substitute
2 teaspoons vegetable oil
1 teaspoon prepared mustard
1½ teaspoons dried dill weed

Preheat oven to 375 degrees. Spray 8 wells of a 12-hole muffin pan with butter-flavored cooking spray or line with paper liners. In a large bowl, combine baking mix, Swiss cheese, and Sugar Twin. In a small bowl, combine skim milk, egg, vegetable oil, mustard, and dill weed. Add milk mixture to baking mix mixture. Mix just until combined. Evenly spoon batter into prepared muffin wells. Bake for 24 to 28 minutes or until a toothpick inserted in center comes out clean. Remove muffins from pan immediately and place on a wire rack to cool.

Each serving equals:

HE: 1 Bread • ¾ Protein • ¼ Fat •
8 Optional Calories

150 Calories • 6 gm Fat • 6 gm Protein •
18 gm Carbohydrate • 494 mg Sodium •
49 mg Calcium • 0 gm Fiber

DIABETIC: 1 Starch • 1 Meat

Pronto Pizza Muffins

Are your kids such fans of pizza that they would happily eat it any-time? Well, I'm not suggesting you serve these delights at 8 in the morning, but you *could*! Instead of tossing cheese into the skillet along with the eggs, why not bake a batch of these?

○ Serves 8

¾ cup Yoplait plain fat-free yogurt
⅓ cup Carnation Nonfat Dry Milk Powder
1 egg or equivalent in egg substitute
1 cup (one 8-ounce can) Hunt's Tomato Sauce
1 teaspoon Italian seasoning
⅔ cup (2¼ ounces) shredded Kraft reduced-fat mozzarella cheese
1½ cups all-purpose flour
2 teaspoons baking powder
1 teaspoon baking soda

Preheat oven to 400 degrees. Spray 8 wells of a 12-hole muffin pan with olive oil–flavored cooking spray or line with paper liners. In a large bowl, combine yogurt and dry milk powder. Add egg and tomato sauce. Mix well to combine. Stir in Italian seasoning and moz-zarella cheese. In a small bowl, combine flour, baking powder, and baking soda. Add flour mixture to yogurt mixture. Mix gently just to combine. Evenly spoon batter into prepared muffin wells. Bake for 20 to 25 minutes or until a toothpick inserted in center comes out clean. Place muffin pan on a wire rack and let set for 5 minutes. Remove muffins from pan and continue cooling on wire rack.

Each serving equals:

HE: 1 Bread • ½ Protein • ½ Vegetable • ¼ Skim Milk

---

146 Calories • 2 gm Fat • 8 gm Protein • 24 gm Carbohydrate • 557 mg Sodium • 207 mg Calcium • 1 gm Fiber

---

DIABETIC: 1 Starch • ½ Meat • ½ Vegetable

Summer Garden Muffins

Here's a fun way to celebrate just how rosy-ripe your tomatoes are this summer! But if your plants aren't producing just yet, pick up some tomatoes at the farmers' market or even the grocery store, and stir these up tonight! They're wonderful served with a big fresh salad for a light supper. ☻ Serves 8

1½ cups Bisquick Reduced Fat Baking Mix

1 teaspoon dried basil

¼ cup pourable Sugar Twin

¼ cup (¾ ounce) grated Kraft fat-free Parmesan cheese

6 tablespoons skim milk

2 tablespoons Kraft Fat Free Italian Dressing

1 egg or equivalent in egg substitute

¾ cup peeled and finely chopped fresh tomatoes

¼ cup finely chopped onion

Preheat oven to 400 degrees. Spray 8 wells of a 12-hole muffin pan with butter-flavored cooking spray or line with paper liners. In a large bowl, combine baking mix, basil, Sugar Twin, and Parmesan cheese. In a small bowl, combine skim milk, Italian dressing, and egg. Add milk mixture to baking mix mixture. Mix just until combined. Stir in tomatoes and onion. Fill prepared muffin wells ¾ full. Bake for 15 to 20 minutes or until a toothpick inserted in center comes out clean. Place muffin pan on a wire rack and let set for 5 minutes. Remove muffins from pan and continue cooling on wire rack.

Each serving equals:

HE: 1 Bread • ¼ Protein • ¼ Vegetable • 9 Optional Calories

---

110 Calories • 2 gm Fat • 3 gm Protein • 20 gm Carbohydrate • 355 mg Sodium • 41 mg Calcium • 1 gm Fiber

---

DIABETIC: 1 Starch • ½ Fat

Oh-So-Quick Breads

Have you ever said, "I love the taste of homemade bread, but I just haven't got the time or the patience to make it"? True, traditional yeast breads take a lot of time to rise and require kneading. And bread machines take up a lot of counter space, which is why so many of them have been relegated to the garage—or the yard sale.

The quick bread is the perfect solution!

All you need is a loaf pan, a warm oven, a few ingredients, and about an hour's baking time (during which you can relax, catch up on your reading, weed your garden, and enjoy your family!).

Quick breads make delightful holiday gifts, but they're definitely not just for special occasions. Most of them freeze beautifully and make great take-alongs for picnics and brown-bag lunches. They're nutritious, they're filling, and they're so reliable that even inexperienced bakers can be proud of the results.

Here's a useful quick-bread tip: If your fruited quick bread comes out a bit too moist, or if it's somewhat dried out and past its prime, slice it, put the slices on a baking sheet, and bake them at a low temperature (250 degrees is good) for about an hour, turning them halfway. Now you have something really wonderful to serve your family or enjoy all by yourself: oven-toasted fruit bread.

What's also wonderful about quick breads (besides how speedily they can be stirred up and baked) is how diverse and varied their flavors can be. If you've got some bananas on your kitchen counter about to turn black, you're blessed with the ingredients for any of my banana breads. (Give **Banana Plantation Walnut Bread** a try!) No fruit in the house except for a few apples on the bottom shelf of your fridge? Don't despair; just put up a pot of your favorite coffee and stir up my **Coffee's On! Apple Bread.** And if you want to win a round of applause from your card club, I promise you that **Chips Ajoy Loaf Bread** will do the trick!

Oh-So-Quick Breads

Walnut Spice Bread

Spice breads and cakes are among my husband Cliff's favorite baked treats, so I enjoy coming up with tasty new variations as often as I can. This nutty dream is downright delightful served warm, with a glass of milk, but it's also terrific enjoyed a day later.

○ Serves 8 (1 thick or 2 thin slices)

½ teaspoon ground cinnamon
½ cup pourable Sugar Twin ☆
⅓ cup Carnation Nonfat Dry Milk Powder
¾ cup water
1 teaspoon white vinegar
1½ cups all-purpose flour
1 (4-serving) package JELL-O sugar-free instant vanilla pudding mix
1 teaspoon baking powder
½ teaspoon baking soda
¼ cup (1 ounce) chopped walnuts
¾ cup Yoplait plain fat-free yogurt
1 egg or equivalent in egg substitute
1 teaspoon vanilla extract

Preheat oven to 375 degrees. Spray a 9-by-5-inch loaf pan with butter-flavored cooking spray. In another small bowl, combine cinnamon and ¼ cup Sugar Twin. Set aside. In a small bowl, combine dry milk powder, water, and vinegar. Set aside. In a large bowl, combine flour, dry pudding mix, remaining ¼ cup Sugar Twin, baking powder, baking soda, and walnuts. Stir yogurt, egg, and vanilla extract into milk mixture. Add milk mixture to flour mixture. Mix gently to combine. Evenly spread half of batter into prepared loaf pan. Sprinkle half of cinnamon mixture evenly over top. Repeat layer of remaining batter and cinnamon mixture. Bake for 50 to 55 minutes or until a toothpick inserted in center comes out clean. Place loaf pan on a wire rack and let set for 10 minutes. Remove bread from pan and continue cooling on wire rack. Cut into 8 thick or 16 thin slices.

Each serving equals:

HE: 1 Bread • ¼ Skim Milk • ¼ Protein • ¼ Fat •
19 Optional Calories

---

151 Calories • 3 gm Fat • 6 gm Protein •
25 gm Carbohydrate • 345 mg Sodium •
128 mg Calcium • 1 gm Fiber

DIABETIC: 1½ Starch • 1 Fat

Coffee's On! Apple Bread

"That coffee's cold," one of my staff noted as I began to pour out a cup. I just smiled and added it to the batter for this sure-to-become-a-classic quick bread. I can't tell you *why* the coffee brings out something special in the apple flavor, but I can promise you it does!

○ Serves 8 (1 thick or 2 thin slices)

1½ cups all-purpose flour
1 (4-serving) package JELL-O sugar-free instant vanilla pudding
    mix
½ cup pourable Sugar Twin
1 teaspoon baking powder
½ teaspoon baking soda
1 teaspoon apple pie spice
1½ cups (3 small) cored, unpeeled, and finely chopped cooking
    apples
½ cup raisins
¼ cup (1 ounce) chopped walnuts
½ cup unsweetened applesauce
1 egg or equivalent in egg substitute
⅔ cup cold coffee
1 teaspoon vanilla extract

Preheat oven to 375 degrees. Spray a 9-by-5-inch loaf pan with butter-flavored cooking spray. In a large bowl, combine flour, dry pudding mix, Sugar Twin, baking powder, baking soda, and apple pie spice. Add apples, raisins, and walnuts. Mix well to combine. In a small bowl, combine applesauce, egg, coffee, and vanilla extract. Add applesauce mixture to flour mixture. Mix well to combine. Evenly spread batter into prepared loaf pan. Bake for 1 hour or until a toothpick inserted in center comes out clean. Place loaf pan on a wire rack and let set for 5 minutes. Remove bread from pan and continue cooling on wire rack. Cut into 8 thick or 16 thin slices.

Each serving equals:

HE: 1 Bread • 1 Fruit • ¼ Protein • ¼ Fat •
18 Optional Calories

179 Calories • 3 gm Fat • 4 gm Protein •
34 gm Carbohydrate • 315 mg Sodium •
50 mg Calcium • 2 gm Fiber

DIABETIC: 1 Starch • 1 Fruit • ½ Fat

Blueberry Paradise Bread

Those fresh, ripe, oh-so-sweet blueberries at the height of summer just seem to plead to be baked into something yummy. Stirring them into a traditional banana bread recipe transformed an everyday eating pleasure into something spectacular!

☺ Serves 8 (1 thick or 2 thin slices)

1½ cups all-purpose flour
1 (4-serving) package JELL-O
    sugar-free instant
    banana cream pudding
    mix
¼ cup pourable Sugar Twin
1 teaspoon baking powder
½ teaspoon baking soda
⅔ cup (2 ripe medium)
    mashed bananas

1 teaspoon vanilla extract
½ cup unsweetened applesauce
1 egg or equivalent in egg
    substitute
¾ cup blueberries
¼ cup (1 ounce) chopped
    walnuts

Preheat oven to 375 degrees. Spray a 9-by-5-inch loaf pan with butter-flavored cooking spray. In a large bowl, combine flour, dry pudding mix, Sugar Twin, baking powder, and baking soda. In a small bowl, combine bananas, vanilla extract, applesauce, and egg. Fold in blueberries and walnuts. Add banana mixture to flour mixture. Mix just until combined. Evenly spread batter into prepared loaf pan. Bake for 50 to 55 minutes or until a toothpick inserted in center comes out clean. Place loaf pan on a wire rack and let set for 10 minutes. Remove bread from pan and continue cooling on wire rack. Cut into 8 thick or 16 thin slices.

Each serving equals:

HE: 1 Bread • ¾ Fruit • ¼ Protein • ¼ Fat •
16 Optional Calories

155 Calories • 3 gm Fat • 4 gm Protein •
28 gm Carbohydrate • 320 mg Sodium •
46 mg Calcium • 2 gm Fiber

DIABETIC: 1 Starch • 1 Fruit • ½ Fat

Orange–Poppy Seed Bread

Poppy seeds are what I call a "team player"—on their own, they don't seem to have much flavor, but when they're combined with other ingredients (in this case, the orange juice and applesauce) and baked, they bring out the best in the rest!

● Serves 8 (1 thick or 2 thin slices)

> 1½ cups all-purpose flour
> 1 (4-serving) package JELL-O sugar-free instant vanilla pudding mix
> ¼ cup pourable Sugar Twin
> 1 teaspoon baking powder
> ½ teaspoon baking soda
> 1 tablespoon poppy seeds
> ¾ cup unsweetened orange juice
> ¼ cup unsweetened applesauce
> 2 tablespoons vegetable oil
> 1 teaspoon vanilla extract

Preheat oven to 375 degrees. Spray a 9-by-5-inch loaf pan with butter-flavored cooking spray. In a large bowl, combine flour, dry pudding mix, Sugar Twin, baking powder, baking soda, and poppy seeds. In a small bowl, combine orange juice, applesauce, vegetable oil, and vanilla extract. Add orange juice mixture to flour mixture. Mix gently to combine. Evenly spread batter into prepared loaf pan. Bake for 40 to 50 minutes or until a toothpick inserted in center comes out clean. Place loaf pan on a wire rack and let set for 5 minutes. Remove bread from pan and continue cooling on wire rack. Cut into 8 thick or 16 thin slices.

Each serving equals:

HE: 1 Bread • ¾ Fat • ¼ Fruit • 16 Optional Calories

126 Calories • 2 gm Fat • 3 gm Protein •
24 gm Carbohydrate • 306 mg Sodium •
55 mg Calcium • 1 gm Fiber

DIABETIC: 1½ Starch/Carbohydrate

Coconut-Apricot Loaf Bread

I go through a lot of extracts in my test kitchen—probably because they lend so much rich flavor to my Healthy Exchanges goodies without adding extra calories or fat. This bread is chock-full of nuts and fruit, and when you add a touch of coconut, you're ready to celebrate just about anything. ○ Serves 8 (1 thick or 2 thin slices)

1½ cups Bisquick Reduced Fat Baking Mix

1 (4-serving) package JELL-O sugar-free instant vanilla pudding mix

¼ cup Brown Sugar Twin ☆

1 teaspoon baking powder

½ teaspoon baking soda

¼ cup (1 ounce) chopped pecans

⅔ cup (3 ounces) chopped dried apricots

¼ cup flaked coconut ☆

⅓ cup Yoplait plain fat-free yogurt

⅓ cup Kraft fat-free mayonnaise

¾ cup water

2 teaspoons coconut extract

Preheat oven to 375 degrees. Spray a 9-by-5-inch loaf pan with butter-flavored cooking spray. In a large bowl, combine baking mix, dry pudding mix, 2 tablespoons Brown Sugar Twin, baking powder, and baking soda. Stir in pecans, apricots, and 2 tablespoons coconut. In a medium bowl, combine yogurt, mayonnaise, water, and coconut extract. Add yogurt mixture to baking mix mixture. Mix gently to combine. Evenly spread batter into prepared loaf pan. In a small bowl, combine remaining 2 tablespoons coconut and remaining 2 tablespoons Brown Sugar Twin. Sprinkle mixture evenly over batter. Bake for 45 to 55 minutes or until a toothpick inserted in center comes out clean. Place loaf pan on a wire rack and let set for 5 minutes. Remove bread from pan and continue cooling on wire rack. Cut into 8 thick or 16 thin slices.

Each serving equals:

HE: 1 Bread • ½ Fruit • ½ Fat • ¼ Slider •
13 Optional Calories

168 Calories • 4 gm Fat • 3 gm Protein •
30 gm Carbohydrate • 666 mg Sodium •
77 mg Calcium • 2 gm Fiber

DIABETIC: 1½ Starch/Carbohydrate • ½ Fruit • ½ Fat

Pineapple-Raisin Bread

No grandma gets to see her beloved grandkids as often as she'd like, but that doesn't mean she isn't thinking about them when they're not around. This recipe was surely inspired by my growing-up-fast grandson Josh, who adores pineapple.

○ Serves 8 (1 thick or 2 thin slices)

1½ cups all-purpose flour
½ cup pourable Sugar Twin
1 teaspoon baking powder
½ teaspoon baking soda
⅓ cup unsweetened
    applesauce
1 egg or equivalent in egg
    substitute

1 cup (one 8-ounce can)
    crushed pineapple, packed
    in fruit juice, undrained
¼ cup (1 ounce) chopped
    walnuts
6 tablespoons raisins

Preheat oven to 375 degrees. Spray a 9-by-5-inch loaf pan with butter-flavored cooking spray. In a medium bowl, combine flour, Sugar Twin, baking powder, and baking soda. In a small bowl, combine applesauce, egg, and undrained pineapple. Add applesauce mixture to flour mixture. Mix just until combined. Stir in walnuts and raisins. Evenly spread batter into prepared loaf pan. Bake for 50 to 60 minutes or until a toothpick inserted in center comes out clean. Place loaf pan on a wire rack and let set for 10 minutes. Remove bread from pan and continue cooling on wire rack. Cut into 8 thick or 16 thin slices.

Each serving equals:

HE: 1 Bread • ⅔ Fruit • ¼ Protein • ¼ Fat •
6 Optional Calories

163 Calories • 3 gm Fat • 4 gm Protein •
30 gm Carbohydrate • 150 mg Sodium •
52 mg Calcium • 2 gm Fiber

DIABETIC: 1 Starch • 1 Fruit • ½ Fat

Cranberry-Orange Nut Bread

This has become one of my favorite combinations in the past few years. (I'm not the only fan, either—Ben & Jerry invented a popular sorbet blending them!) And did you know that walnuts, naturally low in fat, are a truly heart-healthy food?

● Serves 8 (1 thick or 2 thin slices)

1½ cups all-purpose flour	¼ cup unsweetened orange
½ cup pourable Sugar Twin	juice
1 teaspoon baking powder	¼ cup unsweetened applesauce
¼ teaspoon baking soda	¼ cup Land O Lakes no-fat
1 cup finely chopped fresh or	sour cream
frozen cranberries	1 egg, slightly beaten, or
¼ cup (1 ounce) chopped	equivalent in egg
walnuts	substitute

Preheat oven to 375 degrees. Spray a 9-by-5-inch loaf pan with butter-flavored cooking spray. In a large bowl, combine flour, Sugar Twin, baking powder, and baking soda. Stir in cranberries and walnuts. In a small bowl, combine orange juice, applesauce, sour cream, and egg. Add orange juice mixture to flour mixture. Mix just until combined. Evenly spread batter into prepared loaf pan. Bake for 55 to 65 minutes or until a toothpick inserted in center comes out clean. Place loaf pan on a wire rack and let set for 5 minutes. Remove bread from pan and continue cooling on wire rack. Cut into 8 thick or 16 thin slices.

Each serving equals:

HE: 1 Bread • ¼ Protein • ¼ Fruit • ¼ Fat • 14 Optional Calories

135 Calories • 3 gm Fat • 4 gm Protein • 23 gm Carbohydrate • 119 mg Sodium • 54 mg Calcium • 1 gm Fiber

DIABETIC: 1½ Starch/Carbohydrate • ½ Fat

Peach-Walnut Bread

Suppose you wake up some Sunday morning thinking about how good homemade bread would taste. But—phooey—you don't have any fresh fruit in the house. No problem! Here's a pantry pleaser made with canned peaches and raisins that will warm your heart and soothe your soul. ☻ Serves 8 (1 thick or 2 thin slices)

1½ cups all-purpose flour
1 (4-serving) package JELL-O sugar-free instant vanilla pudding mix
¼ cup pourable Sugar Twin
1 teaspoon baking powder
½ teaspoon baking soda
½ cup raisins
¼ cup (1 ounce) chopped walnuts
⅔ cup Carnation Nonfat Dry Milk Powder
½ cup water
1 egg or equivalent in egg substitute
1 teaspoon vanilla extract
1 cup (one 8-ounce can) sliced peaches, packed in fruit juice, undrained and finely chopped

Preheat oven to 375 degrees. Spray a 9-by-5-inch loaf pan with butter-flavored cooking spray. In a large bowl, combine flour, dry pudding mix, Sugar Twin, baking powder, and baking soda. Stir in raisins and walnuts. In a small bowl, combine dry milk powder and water. Add egg and vanilla extract. Mix well to combine. Stir in undrained peaches. Add milk mixture to flour mixture. Mix gently to combine. Evenly spread batter into prepared loaf pan. Bake for 55 to 65 minutes or until a toothpick inserted in center comes out clean. Place loaf pan on a wire rack and let set for 5 minutes. Remove bread from pan and continue cooling on wire rack. Cut into 8 thick or 16 thin slices.

Each serving equals:

HE: 1 Bread • ¾ Fruit • ¼ Skim Milk • ¼ Protein • ¼ Fat • 16 Optional Calories

191 Calories • 3 gm Fat • 6 gm Protein • 35 gm Carbohydrate • 346 mg Sodium • 119 mg Calcium • 2 gm Fiber

DIABETIC: 1 Starch/Carbohydrate • 1 Fruit • ½ Fat

Old-Fashioned Banana Bread

I stirred even more ripe banana than usual into this traditional banana bread because, as Mae West might have said, "Too much of a good thing can be wonderful!" See if you agree!

● Serves 8 (1 thick or 2 thin slices)

½ cup Land O Lakes no-fat sour cream
½ cup pourable Sugar Twin
1 cup (3 ripe medium) mashed bananas
1 egg or equivalent in egg substitute
1½ cups all-purpose flour
1 teaspoon baking powder
½ teaspoon baking soda
¼ cup (1 ounce) chopped walnuts

Preheat oven to 375 degrees. Spray a 9-by-5-inch loaf pan with butter-flavored cooking spray. In a large bowl, combine sour cream and Sugar Twin. Stir in bananas and egg. Add flour, baking powder, and baking soda. Mix gently to combine. Fold in walnuts. Evenly spread batter into prepared loaf pan. Bake for 55 to 65 minutes or until a toothpick inserted in center comes out clean. Place loaf pan on a wire rack and let set for 5 minutes. Remove bread from pan and continue cooling on wire rack. Cut into 8 thick or 16 thin slices.

Each serving equals:

HE: 1 Bread • ¾ Fruit • ¼ Protein • ¼ Fat • ¼ Slider • 1 Optional Calorie

143 Calories • 3 gm Fat • 4 gm Protein • 25 gm Carbohydrate • 186 mg Sodium • 27 mg Calcium • 1 gm Fiber

DIABETIC: 1 Starch • 1 Fruit • ½ Fat

Peanut Butter–Banana Bread

I haven't met a kid yet who didn't love biting into a peanut butter and banana sandwich, so I figured I'd join the party and create a quick bread that satisfies all those big and little kids out there. The tiny bits of chopped nuts give this a great old-fashioned flavor.

○ Serves 8 (1 thick or 2 thin slices)

1½ cups all-purpose flour	⅔ cup (2 ripe medium) mashed
1 (4-serving) package JELL-O sugar-free instant vanilla pudding mix	bananas
	¼ cup Peter Pan reduced-fat peanut butter
1 teaspoon baking powder	1 egg or equivalent in egg
½ teaspoon baking soda	substitute
¼ cup (1 ounce) chopped dry-roasted peanuts	¼ cup water
	1 teaspoon vanilla extract

Preheat oven to 375 degrees. Spray a 9-by-5-inch loaf pan with butter-flavored cooking spray. In a large bowl, combine flour, dry pudding mix, baking powder, and baking soda. Stir in peanuts. In a medium bowl, combine bananas and peanut butter. Stir in egg, water, and vanilla extract. Add banana mixture to flour mixture. Mix just until combined. Evenly spread batter into prepared loaf pan. Bake for 35 to 45 minutes or until a toothpick inserted in center comes out clean. Place loaf pan on a wire rack and let set for 5 minutes. Remove bread from pan and continue cooling on wire rack. Cut into 8 thick or 16 thin slices.

Each serving equals:

HE: 1 Bread • ¾ Protein • ¾ Fat • ½ Fruit • 13 Optional Calories

181 Calories • 5 gm Fat • 6 gm Protein • 28 gm Carbohydrate • 351 mg Sodium • 43 mg Calcium • 2 gm Fiber

DIABETIC: 1 Starch • ½ Meat • ½ Fat • ½ Fruit

Bountiful Blessings Bread

Don't you just love it when you slice off a piece of fresh-baked bread and discover gorgeous little explosions of color inside? That's part of the magic of this scrumptious bread—all those bursts of red in a fragrant and delectable quick bread that's perfect to serve when friends visit. ❤ Serves 8 (1 thick or 2 thin slices)

> 1 cup fresh or frozen cranberries
> ¼ cup water
> 1½ cups all-purpose flour
> 1 (4-serving) package JELL-O sugar-free instant vanilla pudding mix
> ¼ cup pourable Sugar Twin
> 1½ teaspoons baking powder
> ¼ teaspoon baking soda
> ¼ cup (1 ounce) chopped walnuts
> ⅔ cup (2 ripe medium) mashed bananas
> 1 egg or equivalent in egg substitute
> ⅓ cup unsweetened applesauce

Preheat oven to 375 degrees. Spray a 9-by-5-inch loaf pan with butter-flavored cooking spray. In a small saucepan, combine cranberries and water. Cook over medium heat 6 to 8 minutes or until cranberries soften, stirring constantly. Remove saucepan from heat, place on a wire rack, and allow to cool completely. Meanwhile, in a large bowl, combine flour, dry pudding mix, Sugar Twin, baking powder, baking soda, and walnuts. In a small bowl, combine bananas, egg, and applesauce. Stir in cooled cranberry mixture. Add fruit mixture to flour mixture. Mix gently to combine. Evenly spread batter into prepared loaf pan. Bake for 55 to 65 minutes or until a toothpick inserted in center comes out clean. Place loaf pan on a wire rack, and let set for 10 minutes. Remove bread from pan and continue cooling on wire rack. Cut into 8 thick or 16 thin slices.

Each serving equals:

HE: 1 Bread • ⅔ Fruit • ¼ Protein • ¼ Fat •
16 Optional Calories

---

155 Calories • 3 gm Fat • 4 gm Protein •
28 gm Carbohydrate • 305 mg Sodium •
63 mg Calcium • 2 gm Fiber

DIABETIC: 1 Starch • ½ Fruit • ½ Fat

Banana-Pineapple Nut Bread

Here's a pretty bread that bakes up moist and hearty, with lots of fruit flavor and wonderful chunks of my favorite nut—pecans! In summer, why not try baking breads in your toaster oven instead of heating up the whole kitchen? But be sure to adjust your cooking time by checking the bread after 40 minutes.

○ Serves 8 (1 thick or 2 thin slices)

> 1½ cups all-purpose flour
> 1 (4-serving) package JELL-O sugar-free instant banana cream
>   pudding mix
> 1 teaspoon baking powder
> ½ teaspoon baking soda
> ¼ cup (1 ounce) chopped pecans
> 8 maraschino cherries, chopped
> ⅓ cup (1 ripe medium) mashed banana
> 1 cup (one 8-ounce can) crushed pineapple, packed in fruit juice,
>   undrained
> ¼ cup Land O Lakes no-fat sour cream

Preheat oven to 375 degrees. Spray a 9-by-5-inch loaf pan with butter-flavored cooking spray. In a large bowl, combine flour, dry pudding mix, baking powder, and baking soda. Stir in pecans and maraschino cherries. In a small bowl, combine banana, undrained pineapple, and sour cream. Add banana mixture to flour mixture. Mix just until combined. Evenly spread batter into prepared loaf pan. Bake for 55 to 65 minutes or until a toothpick inserted in center comes out clean. Place loaf pan on a wire rack and let set for 5 minutes. Remove bread from pan and continue cooling on wire rack. Cut into 8 thick or 16 thin slices.

Each serving equals:

HE: 1 Bread • ½ Fruit • ½ Fat • ¼ Slider •
10 Optional Calories

---

158 Calories • 2 gm Fat • 3 gm Protein •
32 gm Carbohydrate • 321 mg Sodium •
51 mg Calcium • 1 gm Fiber

DIABETIC: 1 Starch • 1 Fruit • ½ Fat

Banana Plantation Walnut Bread

Imagine how lovely it would be to sit on a wide verandah (just like those in *Gone With the Wind*), nibble on this bread, and chat with friends! Even if your lifestyle is anything but leisurely, you can enjoy this tasty bread and relax for a few minutes at least!

♥ Serves 8 (1 thick or 2 thin slices)

> 1 cup + 2 tablespoons all-purpose flour
> ¼ cup (¾ ounce) quick oats
> 1 (4-serving) package JELL-O sugar-free instant pistachio pudding mix
> ¼ cup pourable Sugar Twin
> 1 egg, beaten, or equivalent in egg substitute
> ⅔ cup (2 ripe medium) mashed bananas
> 1 cup (one 8-ounce can) crushed pineapple, packed in fruit juice, undrained
> 1 teaspoon baking soda
> ¼ cup warm water
> ¼ cup (1 ounce) chopped walnuts

Preheat oven to 325 degrees. Spray a 9-by-5-inch loaf pan with butter-flavored cooking spray. In a large bowl, combine flour, oats, dry pudding mix, and Sugar Twin. In a medium bowl, combine beaten egg, bananas, and undrained pineapple. In a small bowl, dissolve baking soda in warm water. Stir into banana mixture. Add banana mixture to flour mixture. Mix well to combine. Fold in walnuts. Evenly spread batter into prepared loaf pan. Bake for 55 to 60 minutes or until a toothpick inserted in center comes out clean. Place loaf pan on a wire rack and let set for 5 minutes. Remove bread from pan and continue cooling on wire rack. Cut into 8 thick or 16 thin slices.

HINT: Pistachio nuts may be used in place of walnuts.

Each serving equals:

HE: 1 Bread • ¾ Fruit • ¼ Protein • ¼ Fat •
16 Optional Calories

---

151 Calories • 3 gm Fat • 4 gm Protein •
27 gm Carbohydrate • 326 mg Sodium •
16 mg Calcium • 1 gm Fiber

DIABETIC: 1 Starch • 1 Fruit • ½ Fat

Banana-Pecan Square Bread

I wasn't trying to imply that anyone who enjoys this rich banana bread must be a square, I promise you! Most of my quick breads are baked in a traditional loaf pan, but I thought this one turned out best in an 8-inch square pan. Be as newfangled as you like, and savor this splendid treat. 〇 Serves 8

1½ cups Bisquick Reduced Fat Baking Mix
1 (4-serving) package JELL-O sugar-free instant vanilla pudding
   mix
¼ cup (1 ounce) chopped pecans
⅔ cup (2 ripe medium) mashed bananas
⅓ cup Land O Lakes no-fat sour cream
¼ cup skim milk
1 teaspoon vanilla extract

Preheat oven to 375 degrees. Spray an 8-by-8-inch baking dish with butter-flavored cooking spray. In a large bowl, combine baking mix, dry pudding mix, and pecans. In a medium bowl, combine bananas, sour cream, skim milk, and vanilla extract. Add banana mixture to baking mix mixture. Mix gently just to combine. Evenly spread batter into prepared baking dish. Bake for 25 to 30 minutes or until a toothpick inserted in center comes out clean. Place baking dish on a wire rack and let set for 5 minutes. Cut into 8 servings.

Each serving equals:

HE: 1 Bread • ½ Fruit • ¼ Fat • ¼ Slider •
5 Optional Calories

144 Calories • 4 gm Fat • 3 gm Protein •
24 gm Carbohydrate • 444 mg Sodium •
40 mg Calcium • 0 gm Fiber

DIABETIC: 1 Starch • ½ Fruit • ½ Fat

Jackpot Quick Bread

Getting your vitamins and minerals is already easier when you stir up this appetizing bread! Carrots are rich in vitamin A, and raisins deliver a nice wallop of iron. Did you ever think taking good care of your health would taste this delicious?

● Serves 8 (1 thick or 2 thin slices)

⅔ cup Carnation Nonfat Dry Milk Powder

¾ cup water

2 teaspoons white vinegar

1½ cups all-purpose flour

½ cup pourable Sugar Twin

1½ teaspoons baking powder

1 teaspoon baking soda

1½ teaspoons apple pie spice

½ cup raisins

¼ cup (1 ounce) chopped walnuts

1 cup grated carrots

1 egg or equivalent in egg substitute

¼ cup Kraft fat-free mayonnaise

Preheat oven to 375 degrees. Spray a 9-by-5-inch loaf pan with butter-flavored cooking spray. In a small bowl, combine dry milk powder, water, and vinegar. Set aside. In a large bowl, combine flour, Sugar Twin, baking powder, baking soda, and apple pie spice. Stir in raisins, walnuts, and carrots. Add milk mixture, egg, and mayonnaise to flour mixture. Mix just until combined. Evenly spread batter into prepared loaf pan. Bake for 55 to 65 minutes or until a toothpick inserted in center comes out clean. Place loaf pan on a wire rack and let set for 5 minutes. Remove bread from pan and continue cooling on wire rack. Cut into 8 thick or 16 thin slices.

Each serving equals:

HE: 1 Bread • ½ Fruit • ¼ Skim Milk • ¼ Protein • ¼ Fat • ¼ Vegetable • 11 Optional Calories

175 Calories • 3 gm Fat • 6 gm Protein • 31 gm Carbohydrate • 359 mg Sodium • 138 mg Calcium • 2 gm Fiber

DIABETIC: 1½ Starch/Carbohydrate • ½ Fruit • ½ Fat

Carrots and More Bread

"More" makes me think of added pleasures, not just what you expect when you bite into a piece of carrot bread. Here, "more" means more goodies (nuts, raisins), more flavor (applesauce, vanilla extract), and plenty of spicy goodness (a LOT of cinnamon)! Now, isn't that "more" fun?　　　☺　　Serves 8 (1 thick or 2 thin slices)

> 1½ cups all-purpose flour
> 1 (4-serving) package JELL-O sugar-free instant vanilla pudding
>   mix
> ¼ cup pourable Sugar Twin
> 1 teaspoon baking powder
> ½ teaspoon baking soda
> 1½ teaspoons ground cinnamon
> 1 cup grated carrots
> ½ cup + 2 tablespoons raisins
> ¼ cup (1 ounce) chopped walnuts
> ½ cup unsweetened applesauce
> 1 egg or equivalent in egg substitute
> ⅓ cup skim milk
> 2 teaspoons vegetable oil
> 1 teaspoon vanilla extract

Preheat oven to 375 degrees. Spray a 9-by-5-inch loaf pan with butter-flavored cooking spray. In a large bowl, combine flour, dry pudding mix, Sugar Twin, baking powder, baking soda, and cinnamon. Stir in carrots, raisins, and walnuts. In a small bowl, combine applesauce, egg, skim milk, vegetable oil, and vanilla extract. Add applesauce mixture to flour mixture. Mix gently to combine. Evenly spread batter into prepared loaf pan. Bake for 50 to 60 minutes or until a toothpick inserted in center comes out clean. Place loaf pan on a wire rack and let set for 10 minutes. Remove bread from pan and continue cooling on wire rack. Cut into 8 thick or 16 thin slices.

Each serving equals:

HE: 1 Bread • ¾ Fruit • ½ Fat • ¼ Protein •
¼ Vegetable • 19 Optional Calories

179 Calories • 3 gm Fat • 4 gm Protein •
34 gm Carbohydrate • 317 mg Sodium •
68 mg Calcium • 2 gm Fiber

DIABETIC: 1 Starch • 1 Fruit • ½ Fat

Sunshine Carrot Bread

If ever a food could whisper "Good morning" and urge you to have a great day, it might just be this mouth-watering delight! You'll be amazed to discover what a crispy-sweet top crust this bread delivers.

○ Serves 8 (1 thick or 2 thin slices)

1½ cups all-purpose flour

½ cup + 2 tablespoons pourable Sugar Twin ☆

2 teaspoons baking powder

1 cup finely shredded carrots

6 tablespoons raisins

¼ cup (1 ounce) chopped walnuts

½ cup unsweetened orange juice

1 egg or equivalent in egg substitute

¼ cup Kraft fat-free mayonnaise

Preheat oven to 375 degrees. Spray a 9-by-5-inch loaf pan with butter-flavored cooking spray. In a large bowl, combine flour, ½ cup Sugar Twin, and baking powder. Add carrots, raisins, and walnuts. Mix well to combine. In a medium bowl, combine orange juice, egg, and mayonnaise. Add orange juice mixture to flour mixture. Mix just until combined. Evenly spread batter into prepared loaf pan. Sprinkle remaining 2 tablespoons Sugar Twin evenly over top. Bake for 35 to 45 minutes or until a toothpick inserted in center comes out clean. Place loaf pan on a wire rack and let set for 5 minutes. Remove bread from pan and continue cooling on wire rack. Cut into 8 thick or 16 thin slices.

Each serving equals:

HE: 1 Bread • ½ Fruit • ¼ Protein • ¼ Fat • ¼ Vegetable • 13 Optional Calories

155 Calories • 3 gm Fat • 4 gm Protein • 28 gm Carbohydrate • 202 mg Sodium • 86 mg Calcium • 2 gm Fiber

DIABETIC: 1½ Starch/Carbohydrate • ½ Fruit • ½ Fat

West Coast Carrot Bread

This luscious combination of flavors works beautifully on its own, but this bread would also taste great if spread with just a little fat-free cream cheese (count the few extra calories if you decide to serve it this way).   ○   Serves 8 (1 thick or 2 thin slices)

1½ cups all-purpose flour
½ cup pourable Sugar Twin
1 teaspoon baking powder
1 teaspoon baking soda
1 teaspoon apple pie spice
1 cup finely shredded carrots
¼ cup (1 ounce) chopped walnuts

1 cup (one 8-ounce can) crushed pineapple, packed in fruit juice, undrained
¼ cup Land O Lakes no-fat sour cream
1 teaspoon vanilla extract
1 egg or equivalent in egg substitute

Preheat oven to 375 degrees. Spray a 9-by-5-inch loaf pan with butter-flavored cooking spray. In a large bowl, combine flour, Sugar Twin, baking powder, baking soda, and apple pie spice. Stir in carrots and walnuts. In a small bowl, combine undrained pineapple, sour cream, vanilla extract, and egg. Add pineapple mixture to flour mixture. Mix just until combined. Evenly spread batter into prepared loaf pan. Bake for 55 to 65 minutes or until a toothpick inserted in center comes out clean. Place loaf pan on a wire rack and let set for 5 minutes. Remove bread from pan and continue cooling on wire rack. Cut into 8 thick or 16 thin slices.

Each serving equals:

HE: 1 Bread • ¼ Protein • ¼ Fruit • ¼ Fat •
¼ Vegetable • 14 Optional Calories

147 Calories • 3 gm Fat • 4 gm Protein •
26 gm Carbohydrate • 181 mg Sodium •
26 mg Calcium • 2 gm Fiber

DIABETIC: 1½ Starch/Carbohydrate • ½ Fat

Zucchini-Raisin Bread

You'll notice that I rarely peel the zucchini in my recipes. Why? That little bit of extra fiber adds up to lots of extra-good health, since so many nutrients are lost when veggies and fruit are served without their skin. ☻ Serves 8 (1 thick or 2 thin slices)

1½ cups all-purpose flour
½ cup pourable Sugar Twin
2 teaspoons baking powder
¼ teaspoon baking soda
1 teaspoon apple pie spice
¼ cup (1 ounce) chopped
     walnuts
½ cup + 2 tablespoons raisins

1 cup shredded unpeeled
     zucchini
½ cup unsweetened
     applesauce
1 egg or equivalent in egg
     substitute
1 teaspoon vanilla extract

Preheat oven to 375 degrees. Spray a 9-by-5-inch loaf pan with butter-flavored cooking spray. In a large bowl, combine flour, Sugar Twin, baking powder, baking soda, and apple pie spice. Stir in walnuts, raisins, and zucchini. In a small bowl, combine applesauce, egg, and vanilla extract. Add applesauce mixture to flour mixture. Mix just until combined. Evenly spread batter into prepared loaf pan. Bake for 55 to 65 minutes or until a toothpick inserted in center comes out clean. Place loaf pan on a wire rack and let set for 10 minutes. Remove bread from pan and continue cooling on wire rack. Cut into 8 thick or 16 thin slices.

Each serving equals:

HE: 1 Bread • ¾ Fruit • ¼ Protein • ¼ Fat •
¼ Vegetable • 6 Optional Calories

163 Calories • 3 gm Fat • 4 gm Protein •
30 gm Carbohydrate • 172 mg Sodium •
86 mg Calcium • 2 gm Fiber

DIABETIC: 1 Starch • 1 Fruit • ½ Fat

Zucchini-Orange Bread

It takes time and experience to figure out the right combos of spices in baked goods. That's one of the reasons I really enjoyed creating my line of JO's Spices and experimenting with various blends. This bread's a great example of how the right spice can make a wonderful difference! ☻ Serves 8 (1 thick or 2 thin slices)

1½ cups all-purpose flour
1 (4-serving) package JELL-
    O sugar-free instant
    vanilla pudding mix
¼ cup pourable Sugar Twin
1 teaspoon baking powder
½ teaspoon baking soda
1 teaspoon pumpkin pie spice
¼ cup (1 ounce) chopped
    walnuts

½ cup unsweetened orange
    juice
½ cup unsweetened applesauce
1 egg or equivalent in egg
    substitute
1 cup shredded unpeeled
    zucchini

Preheat oven to 375 degrees. Spray a 9-by-5-inch loaf pan with butter-flavored cooking spray. In a large bowl, combine flour, dry pudding mix, Sugar Twin, baking powder, baking soda, pumpkin pie spice, and walnuts. In a small bowl, combine orange juice, applesauce, and egg. Add orange juice mixture to flour mixture. Mix well to combine. Fold in zucchini. Evenly spread batter into prepared loaf pan. Bake for 45 to 55 minutes or until a toothpick inserted in center comes out clean. Place loaf pan on a wire rack and let set for 10 minutes. Remove bread from pan and continue cooling on wire rack. Cut into 8 thick or 16 thin slices.

Each serving equals:

HE: 1 Bread • ¼ Protein • ¼ Fruit • ¼ Fat •
¼ Vegetable • 16 Optional Calories

143 Calories • 3 gm Fat • 4 gm Protein •
25 gm Carbohydrate • 314 mg Sodium •
48 mg Calcium • 1 gm Fiber

DIABETIC: 1½ Starch/Carbohydrate • ½ Fat

Pumpkin Spice Bread

If you've got a kids' party planned for Halloween, this might be fun to serve. It's got great color and flavor, it's tangy and sweet, and it makes those little tummies feel very happy!

○ Serves 8 (1 thick or 2 thin slices)

> 1½ cups all-purpose flour
> 1 (4-serving) package JELL-O sugar-free instant vanilla pudding mix
> ¼ cup pourable Sugar Twin
> 1½ teaspoons pumpkin pie spice
> 1 teaspoon baking powder
> ½ teaspoon baking soda
> ¼ cup (1 ounce) chopped pecans
> ½ cup raisins
> 2 cups (one 15-ounce can) pumpkin

Preheat oven to 375 degrees. Spray a 9-by-5-inch loaf pan with butter-flavored cooking spray. In a large bowl, combine flour, dry pudding mix, Sugar Twin, pumpkin pie spice, baking powder, and baking soda. Stir in pecans and raisins. Add pumpkin. Mix gently to combine. Evenly spread batter into prepared loaf pan. Bake for 40 to 50 minutes or until a toothpick inserted in center comes out clean. Place loaf pan on a wire rack and let set for 10 minutes. Remove bread from pan and continue cooling on wire rack. Cut into 8 thick or 16 thin slices.

HINT: This is a moist, heavy bread.

Each serving equals:

> HE: 1 Bread • ½ Fruit • ½ Fat • ½ Vegetable • 16 Optional Calories
>
> ---
> 166 Calories • 2 gm Fat • 3 gm Protein • 34 gm Carbohydrate • 309 mg Sodium • 60 mg Calcium • 3 gm Fiber
>
> ---
> DIABETIC: 1½ Starch/Carbohydrate • ½ Fruit • ½ Fat

Sour Cream–Pumpkin Nut Bread ❄

This bread is one of the richest ones I've ever created, and it's also amazingly moist, due in no small part to the fat-free sour cream you stir into the mix. I think this would be a crowd-pleaser for your next PTA meeting or even to offer as your contribution to your favorite charity's bake sale.

○ Serves 16 (1 thick or 2 thin slices)

2¼ cups all-purpose flour
¾ cup pourable Sugar Twin
1 teaspoon baking powder
2 teaspoons baking soda
1½ teaspoons pumpkin pie spice
½ cup (2 ounces) chopped walnuts

2 cups (one 15-ounce can) pumpkin
½ cup Land O Lakes no-fat sour cream
2 tablespoons vegetable oil
2 eggs or equivalent in egg substitute

Preheat oven to 375 degrees. Spray two 9-by-5-inch loaf pans with butter-flavored cooking spray. In a large bowl, combine flour, Sugar Twin, baking powder, baking soda, and pumpkin pie spice. Stir in walnuts. Add pumpkin, sour cream, vegetable oil, and eggs. Mix gently to combine. Evenly spread batter into prepared loaf pans. Bake for 45 to 55 minutes or until a toothpick inserted in center comes out clean. Place loaf pans on a wire rack and let set for 5 minutes. Remove bread from pans and continue cooling on wire rack. Cut each loaf into 8 thick or 16 thin slices.

Each serving equals:

HE: ¾ Bread • ½ Fat • ¼ Protein • ¼ Vegetable • 12 Optional Calories

124 Calories • 4 gm Fat • 4 gm Protein • 18 gm Carbohydrate • 208 mg Sodium • 42 mg Calcium • 2 gm Fiber

DIABETIC: 1½ Starch/Carbohydrate • ½ Fat

Chips Ajoy Loaf Bread

I had fun naming this scrumptious bread, thinking of how sailors shout with joy when they spot land. Your family won't need to hit the water to feel the excitement. Instead, they might just spot this chocolatey bread cooling on the counter and shout, "Chips Ajoy!"

○ Serves 12

2¼ cups Bisquick Reduced Fat Baking Mix

1 (4-serving) package JELL-O sugar-free instant chocolate pudding mix

⅔ cup Carnation Nonfat Dry Milk Powder

¼ cup pourable Sugar Twin

2 tablespoons (½ ounce) mini chocolate chips

¼ cup (1 ounce) chopped walnuts

2 eggs, slightly beaten, or equivalent in egg substitute

¾ cup Yoplait plain fat-free yogurt

½ cup water

2 teaspoons vegetable oil

1 teaspoon vanilla extract

Preheat oven to 375 degrees. Spray a 9-by-5-inch loaf pan with butter-flavored cooking spray. In a large bowl, combine baking mix, dry pudding mix, dry milk powder, Sugar Twin, chocolate chips, and walnuts. In a small bowl, combine eggs, yogurt, water, oil, and vanilla extract. Add the liquid mixture to the dry mixture. Mix gently just to combine. Evenly spread batter into prepared loaf pan. Bake for 45 to 50 minutes or until a toothpick inserted in center comes out clean. Place loaf pan on a wire rack and let set for 10 minutes. Remove bread from pan and continue cooling on wire rack. Cut into 12 slices.

Each serving equals:

HE: 1 Bread • ⅓ Fat • ¼ Skim Milk • ¼ Protein • 18 Optional Calories

149 Calories • 5 gm Fat • 5 gm Protein • 21 gm Carbohydrate • 404 mg Sodium • 75 mg Calcium • 1 gm Fiber

DIABETIC: 1½ Starch • 1 Fat

Grandma Cary's Irish Soda Bread ❄

Unlike traditional quick breads, soda bread is more like regular yeast bread, but it's ready to eat in a much shorter time. How is this possible? Well, I won't go into the specific kitchen chemistry involved, but it has something to do with the baking soda, baking powder, the liquids, and the oven's heat. This old-fashioned bread is sure to become a family favorite!   ☾   Serves 8

⅔ cup Carnation Nonfat
   Dry Milk Powder
1 cup water
2 teaspoons white vinegar
3 cups all-purpose flour

¼ cup pourable Sugar Twin
1 tablespoon baking powder
½ teaspoon baking soda
½ teaspoon salt
1 tablespoon skim milk

Preheat oven to 375 degrees. Spray a 9-inch pie plate with butter-flavored cooking spray. In a small bowl, combine dry milk powder, water, and vinegar. Set aside. In a large bowl, combine flour, Sugar Twin, baking powder, baking soda, and salt. Add milk mixture to flour mixture. Mix well to combine (dough will be sticky). Turn dough out onto a large piece of aluminum foil. Knead about 10 times or until loose flour is incorporated into dough. Shape into an 8-inch round loaf. Place loaf in prepared pie plate. Cut a cross in top of dough with a sharp knife. Brush lightly with skim milk. Bake for 40 to 45 minutes or until loaf is crusty. Lightly spray top with butter-flavored cooking spray. Place pie plate on a wire rack and allow to cool for 5 minutes. Remove loaf from pie plate and continue cooling on wire rack. Cut into 8 servings.

Each serving equals:

HE: 2 Bread • ¼ Skim Milk • 4 Optional Calories

184 Calories • 0 gm Fat • 7 gm Protein •
39 gm Carbohydrate • 428 mg Sodium •
180 mg Calcium • 2 gm Fiber

DIABETIC: 2½ Starch

Tomato-Zucchini Supper Bread

Here's something delightfully different and remarkably satisfying in every single bite! You get your veggies, you get your protein, you get wonderful fresh bread flavor—all in one terrific panful of taste.

● Serves 8

> 1½ cups Bisquick Reduced Fat Baking Mix
> ¼ cup (¾ ounce) grated Kraft fat-free Parmesan cheese
> 1 tablespoon pourable Sugar Twin
> 1 teaspoon Italian seasoning
> 2 teaspoons dried onion flakes
> 1 teaspoon dried parsley flakes
> 1 cup finely shredded unpeeled zucchini
> 1 cup finely chopped fresh tomato
> 2 tablespoons Heinz Light Harvest Ketchup or any reduced-sodium ketchup
> 2 tablespoons water
> ¼ cup Kraft fat-free mayonnaise
> 1 egg or equivalent in egg substitute
> ⅓ cup (1½ ounces) shredded Kraft reduced-fat Cheddar cheese

Preheat oven to 375 degrees. Spray an 8-by-8-inch baking dish with butter-flavored cooking spray. In a large bowl, combine baking mix, Parmesan cheese, Sugar Twin, Italian seasoning, onion flakes, and parsley flakes. Stir in zucchini and tomato. Add ketchup, water, mayonnaise, and egg. Mix well to combine. Evenly spread batter into prepared baking dish. Bake for 40 minutes. Sprinkle Cheddar cheese evenly over top. Continue baking for 15 to 20 minutes or until a toothpick inserted in center comes out clean. Place baking dish on a wire rack and allow to cool completely. Cut into 8 servings.

Each serving equals:

HE: 1 Bread • ½ Protein • ½ Vegetable •
10 Optional Calories

127 Calories • 3 gm Fat • 4 gm Protein •
21 gm Carbohydrate • 449 mg Sodium •
60 mg Calcium • 1 gm Fiber

DIABETIC: 1½ Starch/Carbohydrate • ½ Vegetable

Cheddar Garden Biscuit Bread

I was thinking about biscuits when I created this recipe, but I wanted the ease of baking just one bread instead of cutting out circles of dough. This dish is cheesy and creamy, full of good-for-you bits of veggies that add so much color and flavor, you'll cheer! My daughter-in-law Pam told me she'd serve this with pleasure.

☻ Serves 8

> 1½ cups Bisquick Reduced Fat Baking Mix
> ¾ cup (3 ounces) shredded Kraft reduced-fat Cheddar cheese
> ½ cup skim milk
> ¼ cup Land O Lakes no-fat sour cream
> 1 cup shredded carrots
> ¾ cup finely chopped unpeeled zucchini
> ¼ cup finely chopped onion

Preheat oven to 375 degrees. Spray an 8-by-8-inch baking dish with butter-flavored cooking spray. In a large bowl, combine baking mix, Cheddar cheese, skim milk, and sour cream. Stir in carrots, zucchini, and onion. Evenly spread batter into prepared baking dish. Bake for 30 to 35 minutes or until a toothpick inserted in center comes out clean. Place baking dish on a wire rack and let set for at least 15 minutes. Cut into 8 servings.

Each serving equals:

> HE: 1 Bread • ½ Protein • ½ Vegetable •
> 13 Optional Calories
>
> ---
>
> 131 Calories • 3 gm Fat • 6 gm Protein •
> 20 gm Carbohydrate • 374 mg Sodium •
> 122 mg Calcium • 1 gm Fiber
>
> ---
>
> DIABETIC: 1 Starch • ½ Meat • ½ Vegetable

Sour Cream–Cheese Bread

Talk about decadent and you might be talking about this luscious dish that's perfect for brunch or supper. It's quick to fix, jammed with creamy flavor, and fills your house with a scrumptious aroma. Try it soon! ☯ Serves 8

1½ cups Bisquick Reduced Fat Baking Mix
¾ cup (3 ounces) shredded Kraft reduced-fat Cheddar cheese
1 teaspoon dried onion flakes
1 teaspoon dried parsley flakes
¾ cup Land O Lakes no-fat sour cream
⅓ cup skim milk

Preheat oven to 375 degrees. Spray an 8-by-8-inch baking dish with butter-flavored cooking spray. In a large bowl, combine baking mix, Cheddar cheese, onion flakes, and parsley flakes. Add sour cream and skim milk. Mix gently to combine. Evenly spread batter into prepared baking dish. Bake for 25 to 30 minutes or until a toothpick inserted in center comes out clean. Place baking dish on a wire rack and let set for at least 15 minutes. Cut into 8 servings.

Each serving equals:

HE: 1 Bread • ½ Protein • ¼ Slider •
6 Optional Calories

131 Calories • 3 gm Fat • 5 gm Protein •
21 gm Carbohydrate • 385 mg Sodium •
123 mg Calcium • 0 gm Fiber

DIABETIC: 1½ Starch

Delectable Coffeecakes

There's probably no baked item that says "Welcome" more warmly than a coffeecake served up fresh from the oven to a gathering of good friends. You start "eating it" with your eyes long before your fork even touches the cake, and the stress and cares of daily life vanish after the very first bite.

If you've never made your own coffeecake, I hope this section of recipes will give you the encouragement you need to do it. I first learned to make coffeecake by watching my grandmother prepare her special ones for the boarders (who always seemed to wake up in plenty of time for breakfast at her boarding house). She was a truly creative baker who varied her recipes depending on what fruits looked really ripe and good. She always seemed inspired by the season as well.

This is a great recipe category for following your heart and topping your cake with the ingredients that make you and your family happiest. Perhaps you'll decide to add some smiles to the grayest winter day by serving cozy and luscious **Applesauce Raisin Coffeecake.** Or take a mini-vacation to Hawaii and save *lots* on the airfare by stirring up **Waikiki Coffeecake!** I bet my son James would drive all the way to DeWitt from Iowa City in a rainstorm for a piece of **Chocolate Chip–Cherries Jubilee Coffeecake**—but he won't have to, since I've shared the recipe with him and Pam already!

Delectable Coffeecakes

Morning Sunshine Coffeecake

It's gray and cloudy—too early to open your eyes, let alone go to work. What you need is a blast of warmth and a little get-up-and-go! You'll get all that and more in this festive and cozy cake.

○ Serves 8

½ cup Brown Sugar Twin
2 teaspoons ground
    cinnamon
1½ cups + 2 tablespoons all-
    purpose flour ☆
1 tablespoon + 1 teaspoon
    reduced-calorie
    margarine, melted
¼ cup (1 ounce) chopped
    walnuts

½ cup pourable Sugar Twin
1 teaspoon baking powder
1 teaspoon baking soda
¼ cup Kraft fat-free
    mayonnaise
1 egg, beaten, or equivalent in
    egg substitute
½ cup skim milk

Preheat oven to 375 degrees. Spray an 8-by-8-inch baking dish with butter-flavored cooking spray. In a large bowl, combine Brown Sugar Twin, cinnamon, and 2 tablespoons flour. Add melted margarine and walnuts. Mix well to combine. Set aside. In another large bowl, combine remaining 1½ cups flour, Sugar Twin, baking powder, and baking soda. Add mayonnaise, egg, and skim milk. Mix just until combined. Evenly spread half of batter into prepared baking dish. Sprinkle walnut mixture evenly over batter. Spread remaining batter over top. Bake for 20 to 25 minutes or until a toothpick inserted in center comes out clean. Place baking dish on a wire rack and let set for at least 15 minutes. Cut into 8 servings.

Each serving equals:

HE: 1 Bread • ½ Fat • ¼ Protein • ¼ Slider •
4 Optional Calories

135 Calories • 3 gm Fat • 4 gm Protein •
23 gm Carbohydrate • 274 mg Sodium •
137 mg Calcium • 1 gm Fiber

DIABETIC: 1½ Starch • ½ Fat

School Bell Coffeecake

Having trouble getting your kids out of bed on time and ready for school? I recommend this easy breakfast delight that celebrates those kid-pleasing flavors, peanut butter and jelly! You won't even need to ring a bell to bring them running to the table!

○ Serves 8

> 1½ cups Bisquick Reduced Fat Baking Mix
> 2 tablespoons pourable Sugar Twin
> ¼ cup Peter Pan reduced-fat peanut butter
> ¼ cup Land O Lakes no-fat sour cream
> ½ cup skim milk
> ½ cup grape spreadable fruit

Preheat oven to 375 degrees. Spray an 8-by-8-inch baking dish with butter-flavored cooking spray. In a large bowl, combine baking mix and Sugar Twin. Add peanut butter, sour cream, and skim milk. Mix well to combine. Evenly spread batter into prepared baking dish. In a small bowl, stir spreadable fruit until soft. Using a fork, swirl fruit spread into batter. Bake for 25 to 30 minutes or until a toothpick inserted in center comes out clean. Place baking dish on a wire rack and let set for at least 15 minutes. Cut into 8 servings.

HINT: Substitute any flavor spreadable fruit for grape.

Each serving equals:

HE: 1 Bread • 1 Fruit • ½ Protein • ½ Fat •
15 Optional Calories

176 Calories • 4 gm Fat • 4 gm Protein •
31 gm Carbohydrate • 317 mg Sodium •
45 mg Calcium • 1 gm Fiber

DIABETIC: 1 Starch • 1 Fruit • ½ Fat

Spice-Walnut Coffeecake

I'm so much more of an early riser than Cliff is, but one secret of a happy marriage is being extra considerate of your spouse's differences. I try to make getting up early easier for Cliff by serving him something warm and fresh from the oven. This spicy-nutty combo is one of his favorites! ☻ Serves 8

> 1½ cups Bisquick Reduced Fat Baking Mix
> ¼ cup pourable Sugar Twin
> 1½ teaspoons apple pie spice
> ¼ cup (1 ounce) chopped walnuts
> ½ cup skim milk
> ¼ cup Kraft fat-free mayonnaise
> 1 egg or equivalent in egg substitute

Preheat oven to 375 degrees. Spray an 8-by-8-inch baking dish with butter-flavored cooking spray. In a large bowl, combine baking mix, Sugar Twin, apple pie spice, and walnuts. Add skim milk, mayonnaise, and egg. Mix well to combine. Evenly spread batter into prepared baking dish. Bake for 25 to 30 minutes or until a toothpick inserted in center comes out clean. Place baking dish on a wire rack and let set for at least 15 minutes. Cut into 8 servings.

Each serving equals:

HE: 1 Bread • ¼ Protein • ¼ Fat •
14 Optional Calories

124 Calories • 4 gm Fat • 3 gm Protein •
19 gm Carbohydrate • 342 mg Sodium •
43 mg Calcium • 0 gm Fiber

DIABETIC: 1 Starch • ½ Fat

Chocolate Chip–Cherries Jubilee Coffeecake

I created this pretty treat to honor my son James's birthday, since he's always loved anything made with cherries. (I wonder if his three sons will share his passion for that juicy red fruit. . . .) He thought this was a wonderful start to a very happy day!

● Serves 8

> 1½ cups Bisquick Reduced Fat Baking Mix
> ½ cup pourable Sugar Twin
> 1 cup pitted and coarsely chopped dark sweet or bing cherries
> ¼ cup (1 ounce) mini chocolate chips
> ½ cup Land O Lakes no-fat sour cream
> ¼ cup water
> 1 teaspoon brandy extract

Preheat oven to 375 degrees. Spray an 8-by-8-inch baking dish with butter-flavored cooking spray. In a large bowl, combine baking mix and Sugar Twin. Stir in cherries and chocolate chips. Add sour cream, water, and brandy extract. Mix gently just to combine. Evenly spread batter into prepared baking dish. Bake for 25 to 35 minutes or until a toothpick inserted in center comes out clean. Place baking dish on a wire rack and let set for at least 15 minutes. Cut into 8 servings.

Each serving equals:

> HE: 1 Bread • ¼ Fruit • ¼ Slider •
> 19 Optional Calories
>
> ---
>
> 127 Calories • 3 gm Fat • 2 gm Protein •
> 23 gm Carbohydrate • 282 mg Sodium •
> 38 mg Calcium • 1 gm Fiber
>
> ---
>
> DIABETIC: 1½ Starch/Carbohydrate

Velvet Crumb Coffeecake

A classic coffeecake is always topped with tasty crumbs, and this one is no exception. Close your eyes and imagine a velvety texture in those sweet crumbs, then try a substantial forkful of this morning marvel. Smooth sailing ahead! ◐ Serves 8

> 1½ cups Bisquick Reduced Fat Baking Mix
> ½ cup + 2 tablespoons pourable Sugar Twin ☆
> 1 egg or equivalent in egg substitute
> ¾ cup Yoplait plain fat-free yogurt
> ⅓ cup Carnation Nonfat Dry Milk Powder
> 2 teaspoons vanilla extract
> 2 tablespoons flaked coconut
> ¼ cup (1 ounce) chopped walnuts
> 2 tablespoons Brown Sugar Twin
> 2 tablespoons skim milk
> 1 tablespoon + 1 teaspoon reduced-calorie margarine

Preheat oven to 375 degrees. Spray an 8-by-8-inch baking dish with butter-flavored cooking spray. In a large bowl, combine baking mix, ½ cup Sugar Twin, egg, yogurt, dry milk powder, and vanilla extract. Mix well to combine. Evenly spread batter into prepared baking dish. Bake for 25 to 30 minutes or until a toothpick inserted in center comes out clean. Place baking dish on a wire rack. Meanwhile, set oven setting to Broil. In a medium bowl, combine coconut, walnuts, remaining 2 tablespoons Sugar Twin, Brown Sugar Twin, skim milk, and margarine. Spread crumb mixture evenly over warm coffeecake. Return baking dish to oven and broil for 1 minute or until topping is golden brown. Place baking dish on a wire rack and let set for at least 10 minutes. Cut into 8 servings.

Each serving equals:

HE: 1 Bread • ½ Fat • ¼ Skim Milk • ¼ Protein • 14 Optional Calories

149 Calories • 5 gm Fat • 5 gm Protein • 21 gm Carbohydrate • 315 mg Sodium • 106 mg Calcium • 0 gm Fiber

DIABETIC: 1½ Starch • 1 Fat

Holiday Coffeecake

Can't you just imagine the scene: Your family sits around the table, thrilled to see a luscious coffeecake in front of them, but they're a bit confused—what's the occasion? No birthdays, no anniversaries, and it's not Christmas, so . . . ? Just smile and tell them you've declared a holiday, and enjoy! ☻ Serves 8

> 1½ cups Bisquick Reduced Fat Baking Mix
> ¼ cup pourable Sugar Twin
> ¼ cup (1 ounce) chopped pecans
> 2 tablespoons (½ ounce) mini chocolate chips
> 8 maraschino cherries, quartered
> ¼ cup Land O Lakes no-fat sour cream
> ½ cup skim milk
> 1 teaspoon coconut extract
> 2 tablespoons flaked coconut

Preheat oven to 375 degrees. Spray an 8-by-8-inch baking dish with butter-flavored cooking spray. In a large bowl, combine baking mix and Sugar Twin. Stir in pecans, chocolate chips, and maraschino cherries. Add sour cream, skim milk, and coconut extract. Mix gently to combine. Evenly spread batter into prepared baking dish. Sprinkle coconut evenly over top. Bake for 25 to 30 minutes or until a toothpick inserted in center comes out clean. Place baking dish on a wire rack and let set for at least 15 minutes. Cut into 8 servings.

Each serving equals:

HE: 1 Bread • ½ Fat • ¼ Slider •
19 Optional Calories

145 Calories • 5 gm Fat • 3 gm Protein •
22 gm Carbohydrate • 282 mg Sodium •
47 mg Calcium • 1 gm Fiber

DIABETIC: 1½ Starch/Carbohydrate • ½ Fat

Cinnamon-Orange Coffeecake

Here, I've layered two intense orange "elements," the sweet juice and the rich spreadable fruit. The result: a coffeecake worth grabbing an extra ten minutes for! Just pour another cup of coffee and relax while you enjoy this one! ☻ Serves 8

1 1/2 cups Bisquick Reduced Fat Baking Mix
1/2 cup pourable Sugar Twin
1 teaspoon baking powder
1/2 teaspoon baking soda
1 teaspoon apple pie spice
1 cup unsweetened orange juice
1/2 cup Land O Lakes no-fat sour cream
6 tablespoons orange marmalade spreadable fruit

Preheat oven to 375 degrees. Spray an 8-by-8-inch baking dish with butter-flavored cooking spray. In a large bowl, combine baking mix, Sugar Twin, baking powder, baking soda, and apple pie spice. Add orange juice and sour cream. Mix just until combined. Evenly spread batter into prepared baking dish. Bake for 25 to 30 minutes or until a toothpick inserted in center comes out clean. Place baking dish on a wire rack. Dot top with orange marmalade and spread evenly with a knife. Let set for at least 15 minutes. Cut into 8 servings.

Each serving equals:

HE: 1 Bread • 1 Fruit • 1/4 Slider • 1 Optional Calorie

133 Calories • 1 gm Fat • 2 gm Protein •
29 gm Carbohydrate • 422 mg Sodium •
70 mg Calcium • 0 gm Fiber

DIABETIC: 1 Starch • 1 Fruit

Diamond Head Coffeecake

If you're ever up early enough in Hawaii to watch the sun rise over Diamond Head, you'll see something so beautiful it'll take your breath away. If you'd rather sleep in, you can still get a sense of that magic by enjoying a piece of this splendid cake.   ❍   Serves 8

2 tablespoons Brown Sugar Twin

1 cup (one 8-ounce can) sliced pineapple, packed in fruit juice, drained, and ¼ cup liquid reserved

2 maraschino cherries, halved

1½ cups Bisquick Reduced Fat Baking Mix

1 (4-serving) package JELL-O sugar-free instant vanilla pudding mix

⅔ cup Carnation Nonfat Dry Milk Powder

¼ cup (1 ounce) chopped walnuts

1 egg, beaten, or equivalent in egg substitute

1 cup unsweetened applesauce

1 teaspoon vanilla extract

¼ cup water

Preheat oven to 375 degrees. Spray an 8-by-8-inch baking dish with butter-flavored cooking spray. Evenly sprinkle Brown Sugar Twin over bottom of baking dish. Evenly place pineapple slices on top of Brown Sugar Twin. Place cherry halves in center of pineapple slices, cut side up. In a large bowl, combine baking mix, dry pudding mix, and dry milk powder. Stir in walnuts. In a small bowl, combine egg, applesauce, vanilla extract, reserved pineapple liquid, and water. Add applesauce mixture to baking mix mixture. Mix well to combine. Evenly spread batter over pineapple slices. Bake for 40 to 45 minutes or until a toothpick inserted in center comes out clean. Place baking dish on a wire rack and cool for at least 15 minutes. Cut into 8 servings.

Each serving equals:

HE: 1 Bread • ½ Fruit • ¼ Skim Milk • ¼ Protein •
¼ Fat • 14 Optional Calories

---

180 Calories • 4 gm Fat • 5 gm Protein •
31 gm Carbohydrate • 466 mg Sodium •
99 mg Calcium • 1 gm Fiber

DIABETIC: 1½ Starch • 1 Fat • ½ Fruit

Hawaiian Sunrise Coffeecake

When you live on an island, morning arrives in a very different way than on the wide plains. If you're staying near the water, you'll see the rising sun, all bright and rosy, turning the sea to gold. Aren't we lucky to live in such a beautiful world—and isn't it great that a cake this good is healthy too?　❍　Serves 8

1½ cups Bisquick Reduced
　Fat Baking Mix
¼ cup pourable Sugar Twin
1 cup (one 8-ounce can)
　crushed pineapple,
　packed in fruit juice,
　undrained
⅓ cup Land O Lakes no-fat
　sour cream
⅓ cup unsweetened orange
　juice

1½ teaspoons coconut extract
2 tablespoons purchased graham
　cracker crumbs or
　2 (2½-inch) graham
　cracker squares, made into
　crumbs
2 tablespoons flaked coconut
2 tablespoons (½ ounce)
　chopped pecans

Preheat oven to 375 degrees. Spray an 8-by-8-inch baking dish with butter-flavored cooking spray. In a large bowl, combine baking mix and Sugar Twin. Add undrained pineapple, sour cream, and orange juice. Mix well to combine. Stir in coconut extract. Evenly spread batter into prepared baking dish. In a small bowl, combine graham cracker crumbs, coconut, and pecans. Sprinkle crumb mixture evenly over batter. Bake for 25 to 30 minutes or until a toothpick inserted in center comes out clean. Place baking dish on a wire rack and let set for at least 15 minutes. Cut into 8 servings.

HINT: A self-seal sandwich bag works great for crushing graham
　crackers.

Each serving equals:

HE: 1 Bread • ⅓ Fruit • ¼ Fat • ¼ Slider •
4 Optional Calories

139 Calories • 3 gm Fat • 3 gm Protein •
25 gm Carbohydrate • 289 mg Sodium •
35 mg Calcium • 1 gm Fiber

DIABETIC: 1½ Starch/Carbohydrate • ½ Fat

Piña Colada Coffeecake

In a perfect world, you'd have unlimited vacation time and enough cash to go anywhere you want. Well, unless you're a lottery winner, you probably can't head for the tropics as often as you'd like. But you can eat like a true winner, with this blend of island flavors that makes home sweet home just a little sweeter!

○ Serves 8

> 1½ cups Bisquick Reduced Fat Baking Mix
> ½ cup pourable Sugar Twin
> 1 cup (one 8-ounce can) crushed pineapple, packed in fruit juice, drained, and ⅓ cup liquid reserved
> ¼ cup Land O Lakes no-fat sour cream
> 2 tablespoons water
> 1 teaspoon coconut extract
> 1 teaspoon rum extract
> 2 tablespoons flaked coconut

Preheat oven to 375 degrees. Spray an 8-by-8-inch baking dish with butter-flavored cooking spray. In a large bowl, combine baking mix and Sugar Twin. Add pineapple, reserved pineapple liquid, sour cream, and water. Mix gently just to combine. Stir in coconut extract and rum extract. Evenly spread batter into prepared baking dish. Sprinkle coconut evenly over top. Bake for 30 to 35 minutes or until a toothpick inserted in center comes out clean. Place baking dish on a wire rack and let set for at least 15 minutes. Cut into 8 servings.

Each serving equals:

HE: 1 Bread • ¼ Fruit • 17 Optional Calories		
114 Calories • 2 gm Fat • 2 gm Protein • 22 gm Carbohydrate • 275 mg Sodium • 31 mg Calcium • 1 gm Fiber		
DIABETIC: 1 Starch • 1 Fruit		

Lime-Pineapple Coffeecake

Here's a recipe so utterly simple and yet so spectacular in taste and appearance, it's perfect for anyone with no time to cook! This is truly creamy and luscious, with a blend of flavors that just can't be beat!   ○   Serves 8

> 1½ cups Bisquick Reduced Fat Baking Mix
> 1 (4-serving) package JELL-O sugar-free lime gelatin
> 2 tablespoons (½ ounce) chopped pecans
> 1 cup (one 8-ounce can) crushed pineapple, packed in fruit juice, undrained
> ⅓ cup Land O Lakes no-fat sour cream

Preheat oven to 375 degrees. Spray an 8-by-8-inch baking dish with butter-flavored cooking spray. In a large bowl, combine baking mix, dry gelatin, and pecans. Add undrained pineapple and sour cream. Mix gently just to combine. Evenly spread batter into prepared baking dish. Bake for 20 to 25 minutes or until a toothpick inserted in center comes out clean. Place baking dish on a wire rack and let set for at least 15 minutes. Cut into 8 servings.

Each serving equals:

HE: 1 Bread • ¼ Fruit • ¼ Fat • 15 Optional Calories

135 Calories • 3 gm Fat • 2 gm Protein •
25 gm Carbohydrate • 315 mg Sodium •
39 mg Calcium • 1 gm Fiber

DIABETIC: 1½ Starch/Carbohydrate • ½ Fat

Waikiki Coffeecake

It's the most popular beach on Oahu, and on any given day, it's filled with joyful sunbathers and surfers who wouldn't want to be anywhere else! Well, here's a morning treat that will make you feel just like that, no matter where you happen to live.

● Serves 8

1½ cups Bisquick Reduced Fat Baking Mix

2 tablespoons pourable Sugar Twin

2 tablespoons Brown Sugar Twin

¼ cup (1 ounce) chopped pecans

1 cup (one 8-ounce can) crushed pineapple, packed in fruit juice, undrained

¼ cup Land O Lakes no-fat sour cream

2 teaspoons coconut extract

2 tablespoons flaked coconut

4 maraschino cherries, halved

Preheat oven to 375 degrees. Spray an 8-by-8-inch baking dish with butter-flavored cooking spray. In a large bowl, combine baking mix, Sugar Twin, Brown Sugar Twin, and pecans. Add undrained pineapple, sour cream, and coconut extract. Mix gently just to combine. Evenly spread batter into prepared baking dish. Sprinkle coconut evenly over batter. Arrange cherry halves, cut side down, evenly over top. Bake for 30 to 35 minutes or until a toothpick inserted in center comes out clean. Place baking dish on a wire rack and let set for at least 15 minutes. Cut into 8 servings.

Each serving equals:

HE: 1 Bread • ½ Fat • ¼ Fruit • 19 Optional Calories

144 Calories • 4 gm Fat • 2 gm Protein •
25 gm Carbohydrate • 275 mg Sodium •
32 mg Calcium • 1 gm Fiber

DIABETIC: 1½ Starch/Carbohydrate • ½ Fat

Trade Winds Coffeecake

Ever heard the term "trade winds" but weren't sure what they are? That's what they call the continuous breezes drawing a ship ever closer to the Equator, where warmth is a way of life! If you're feeling the brisk winds of winter or the chill of an early fall, why not think sultry thoughts while savoring a piece of this? ◐ Serves 8

> 1½ cups Bisquick Reduced Fat Baking Mix
> ¼ cup pourable Sugar Twin
> 1 (4-serving) package JELL-O sugar-free instant vanilla pudding mix
> 1 teaspoon ground cinnamon
> ¼ cup (1 ounce) chopped walnuts
> 1 cup unsweetened applesauce
> 1 teaspoon vanilla extract
> 1 egg or equivalent in egg substitute
> 1 cup (one 8-ounce can) crushed pineapple, packed in fruit juice, drained
> ⅓ cup (1 ripe medium) mashed banana

Preheat oven to 375 degrees. Spray an 8-by-8-inch baking dish with butter-flavored cooking spray. In a large bowl, combine baking mix, Sugar Twin, dry pudding mix, cinnamon, and walnuts. Add applesauce, vanilla extract, and egg. Mix well to combine. Stir in pineapple and banana. Evenly spread batter into prepared baking dish. Bake for 35 to 45 minutes or until a toothpick inserted in center comes out clean. Place baking dish on a wire rack and let set for at least 15 minutes. Cut into 8 servings.

Each serving equals:

HE: 1 Bread • ¾ Fruit • ¼ Protein • ¼ Fat • 16 Optional Calories

164 Calories • 4 gm Fat • 3 gm Protein • 29 gm Carbohydrate • 436 mg Sodium • 34 mg Calcium • 1 gm Fiber

DIABETIC: 1 Starch • 1 Fruit • ½ Fat

Luscious Apricot-Walnut Coffeecake

Most of us grow up eating dried apricots, and we don't often get the fresh ones that are like tiny peaches with fuzzy skins. But between those two extremes is the delicious canned variety, which make a splendidly satisfying addition to a classic coffeecake.

○ Serves 8

> 1½ cups all-purpose flour
>
> 2 teaspoons baking powder
>
> ½ teaspoon baking soda
>
> 3 tablespoons pourable Sugar Twin ☆
>
> ⅔ cup Carnation Nonfat Dry Milk Powder
>
> 2 cups (one 16-ounce can) apricots, packed in fruit juice, drained
>   and chopped, and ½ cup liquid reserved
>
> 1 egg or equivalent in egg substitute
>
> 2 teaspoons vanilla extract
>
> 2 tablespoons + 2 teaspoons reduced-calorie margarine
>
> ¼ cup (1 ounce) chopped walnuts
>
> ½ teaspoon ground cinnamon

Preheat oven to 375 degrees. Spray an 8-by-8-inch baking dish with butter-flavored cooking spray. In a large bowl, combine flour, baking powder, baking soda, and 2 tablespoons Sugar Twin. In a medium bowl, combine dry milk powder and reserved apricot liquid. Stir in egg, vanilla extract, and margarine. Mix well using a wire whisk. Add milk mixture to flour mixture. Mix gently just until combined. Fold in apricots and walnuts. Evenly spread batter into prepared baking dish. In a small bowl, combine remaining 1 tablespoon Sugar Twin and cinnamon. Sprinkle cinnamon mixture evenly over batter. Bake for 25 to 35 minutes or until a toothpick inserted in center comes out clean. Place baking dish on a wire rack and let set for at least 10 minutes. Cut into 8 servings.

Each serving equals:

HE: 1 Bread • ¾ Fat • ½ Fruit • ¼ Skim Milk •
¼ Protein • 2 Optional Calories

---

180 Calories • 4 gm Fat • 6 gm Protein •
30 gm Carbohydrate • 182 mg Sodium •
162 mg Calcium • 2 gm Fiber

DIABETIC: 1½ Starch • 1 Fat • ½ Fruit

Cherry-Almond Swirl Coffeecake ❄

Here's one of the most gorgeous coffeecakes I've ever seen, let alone created! Why, mouths were watering in JO's Kitchen Cafe the day we were testing this, and everyone there agreed it was one of the best they'd ever tried! (I made it again for James when he came for a visit with my newest grandchild, Aaron.) ☻   Serves 8

1 (4-serving) package JELL-O sugar-free vanilla cook-and-serve pudding mix
1 (4-serving) package JELL-O sugar-free cherry gelatin
2 cups (one 16-ounce can) tart red cherries, packed in water, drained, and ½ cup liquid reserved

¾ cup water ☆
1 teaspoon almond extract
1½ cups Bisquick Reduced Fat Baking Mix
2 tablespoons pourable Sugar Twin
2 tablespoons (½ ounce) slivered almonds
⅓ cup Land O Lakes no-fat sour cream
¼ cup skim milk

Preheat oven to 375 degrees. Spray an 8-by-8-inch baking dish with butter-flavored cooking spray. In a medium saucepan, combine dry pudding mix, dry gelatin, reserved cherry liquid, and ½ cup water. Stir in cherries. Cook over medium heat until mixture thickens and starts to boil, stirring often, being careful not to crush cherries. Remove from heat. Stir in almond extract. Place saucepan on a wire rack to cool. Meanwhile, in a large bowl, combine baking mix, Sugar Twin, and almonds. Add sour cream, skim milk, and remaining ¼ cup water. Mix gently just to combine. Evenly spread ⅔ of batter into prepared baking dish. Spread cherry mixture evenly over batter. Drop remaining batter by tablespoonful onto cherry mixture. Bake for 20 to 25 minutes or until light brown. Place baking dish on a wire rack and let set for at least 15 minutes. Cut into 8 servings.

Each serving equals:

HE: 1 Bread • ½ Fruit • ¼ Slider •
18 Optional Calories

---

142 Calories • 2 gm Fat • 4 gm Protein •
27 gm Carbohydrate • 368 mg Sodium •
50 mg Calcium • 1 gm Fiber

DIABETIC: 1 Starch • ½ Fruit

Blueberry Coffeecake

I hope you'll take advantage of fresh blueberry season by serving this scrumptious cake for breakfast, for brunch, or for an afternoon card party! It looks as good as it tastes, and it tastes really yummy!

○ Serves 8

> 1 (4-serving) package JELL-O sugar-free vanilla cook-and-serve pudding mix
> 1 (4-serving) package JELL-O sugar-free lemon gelatin
> 1 cup water
> ¾ cup fresh blueberries
> ¼ cup (1 ounce) chopped walnuts
> 1½ cups Bisquick Reduced Fat Baking Mix
> 1 (4-serving) package JELL-O sugar-free instant vanilla pudding mix
> ½ cup unsweetened applesauce
> 1 egg or equivalent in egg substitute
> 1 teaspoon vanilla extract
> ½ cup skim milk

Preheat oven to 375 degrees. Spray an 11-by-7-inch biscuit pan with butter-flavored cooking spray. In a medium saucepan, combine dry cook-and-serve pudding mix, dry gelatin, and water. Cook over medium heat until mixture thickens and starts to boil, stirring constantly. Remove from heat. Gently stir in blueberries and walnuts. Place saucepan on a wire rack to cool. Meanwhile, in a large bowl, combine baking mix and dry instant pudding mix. In a small bowl, combine applesauce, egg, vanilla extract, and skim milk. Add applesauce mixture to baking mix mixture. Mix gently just to combine. Evenly spread ⅔ of batter into prepared biscuit pan. Spread blueberry mixture evenly over batter. Drop remaining batter by tablespoonful over top. Bake for 25 to 35 minutes or until a toothpick inserted in center comes out clean. Place biscuit pan on a wire rack and let set for at least 15 minutes. Cut into 8 servings.

Each serving equals:

HE: 1 Bread • ¼ Protein • ¼ Fruit • ¼ Fat •
¼ Slider • 13 Optional Calories

160 Calories • 4 gm Fat • 4 gm Protein •
27 gm Carbohydrate • 620 mg Sodium •
95 mg Calcium • 1 gm Fiber

DIABETIC: 1½ Starch/Carbohydrate • ½ Fat

Raspberry Mist Coffeecake

If you've got your own raspberry bushes, then you'll probably put this cake on the menu often—or as long as the berries hold out! If you've got to buy them from the market, treat yourself to one of the more luxurious fruits available. You deserve it! ♥ Serves 8

> 1½ cups Bisquick Reduced Fat Baking Mix
> ½ cup pourable Sugar Twin
> ⅓ cup Land O Lakes no-fat sour cream
> ½ cup unsweetened applesauce
> ½ cup Diet Mountain Dew
> ¾ cup fresh red raspberries

Preheat oven to 375 degrees. Spray an 8-by-8-inch baking dish with butter-flavored cooking spray. In a large bowl, combine baking mix and Sugar Twin. Add sour cream, applesauce, and Diet Mountain Dew. Mix gently just to combine. Fold in raspberries. Evenly spread batter into prepared baking dish. Bake for 30 to 40 minutes or until a toothpick inserted in center comes out clean. Place baking dish on a wire rack and let set for at least 15 minutes. Cut into 8 servings.

Each serving equals:

HE: 1 Bread • ¼ Fruit • 16 Optional Calories

101 Calories • 1 gm Fat • 2 gm Protein •
21 gm Carbohydrate • 276 mg Sodium •
32 mg Calcium • 1 gm Fiber

DIABETIC: 1½ Starch/Carbohydrate

Banana-Apricot Coffeecake

Bananas find their way far more often into banana bread than coffeecake, but I thought I'd see how much sweetness and soft texture they might add to a basic coffeecake recipe. The pecans are exactly the right nut for this mix of flavors! ☻ Serves 8

> 1½ cups Bisquick Reduced Fat Baking Mix
> ½ cup pourable Sugar Twin
> ½ teaspoon ground cinnamon
> ⅔ cup (3 ounces) chopped dried apricots
> ¼ cup (1 ounce) chopped pecans
> ⅔ cup (2 ripe medium) mashed bananas
> ¼ cup Land O Lakes no-fat sour cream
> ¼ cup skim milk

Preheat oven to 375 degrees. Spray an 8-by-8-inch baking dish with butter-flavored cooking spray. In a large bowl, combine baking mix, Sugar Twin, and cinnamon. Stir in apricots and pecans. Add bananas, sour cream, and skim milk. Mix gently just to combine. Evenly spread batter into prepared baking dish. Bake for 30 to 40 minutes or until a toothpick inserted in center comes out clean. Place baking dish on a wire rack and let set for at least 15 minutes. Cut into 8 servings.

Each serving equals:

HE: 1 Bread • 1 Fruit • ½ Fat • 16 Optional Calories

152 Calories • 4 gm Fat • 3 gm Protein •
26 gm Carbohydrate • 276 mg Sodium •
43 mg Calcium • 2 gm Fiber

DIABETIC: 1 Starch • 1 Fruit • ½ Fat

Peach Streusel Coffeecake

There's no more old-fashioned and beloved coffeecake than a traditional streusel, with its sweet-and-crunchy topping. I really like the contrast here between the juicy peaches and the crisp oats.

○ Serves 8

> 1½ cups Bisquick Reduced Fat Baking Mix ☆
> 1 (4-serving) package JELL-O sugar-free instant vanilla pudding mix
> ⅔ cup Carnation Nonfat Dry Milk Powder
> ½ teaspoon apple pie spice
> 2 cups (one 16-ounce can) sliced peaches, packed in fruit juice,
>   drained and chopped, and ½ cup liquid reserved
> ⅓ cup water
> 1 teaspoon vanilla extract
> ¼ cup (¾ ounce) quick oats
> 2 tablespoons Brown Sugar Twin
> 2 tablespoons + 2 teaspoons reduced-calorie margarine

Preheat oven to 375 degrees. Spray an 8-by-8-inch baking dish with butter-flavored cooking spray. In a medium bowl, combine 1¼ cups baking mix, dry pudding mix, dry milk powder, and apple pie spice. Add reserved peach liquid, water, and vanilla extract. Mix well to combine. Pour batter into prepared baking dish. Sprinkle peaches evenly over batter. In a small bowl, combine remaining ¼ cup baking mix, oats, and Brown Sugar Twin. Cut in margarine until mixture resembles coarse crumbs. Sprinkle crumb mixture evenly over top. Bake for 25 to 35 minutes or until a toothpick inserted in center comes out clean. Place baking dish on a wire rack and let set for at least 15 minutes. Cut into 8 servings.

Each serving equals:

HE: 1¼ Bread • ½ Fruit • ½ Fat • ¼ Skim Milk •
14 Optional Calories

158 Calories • 2 gm Fat • 4 gm Protein •
31 gm Carbohydrate • 473 mg Sodium •
92 mg Calcium • 1 gm Fiber

DIABETIC: 1½ Starch • ½ Fruit • ½ Fat

Lemon Coffeecake with Blueberry-Coconut Glaze

If you've ever wondered why bakeshop coffeecakes look so irresistible, it's probably the shiny, smooth glazes! Here's a chance to make your own delectably topped cake, and I bet your family will agree it's as lip-smacking yummy as the bakeshop kind! ◔ Serves 8

> 1½ cups Bisquick Reduced Fat Baking Mix
> 1 (4-serving) package JELL-O sugar-free lemon gelatin
> ½ cup Diet Mountain Dew
> ¼ cup Land O Lakes no-fat sour cream
> ½ cup blueberry spreadable fruit
> 1 teaspoon coconut extract
> 2 tablespoons flaked coconut

Preheat oven to 375 degrees. Spray an 8-by-8-inch baking dish with butter-flavored cooking spray. In a large bowl, combine baking mix and dry gelatin. Add Diet Mountain Dew and sour cream. Mix gently just to combine. Evenly spread batter into prepared baking dish. Bake for 20 minutes. In a small bowl, gently stir spreadable fruit with a spoon until soft. Stir in coconut extract. Evenly spread mixture over partially baked coffeecake. Sprinkle coconut evenly over top. Continue baking for 5 minutes or until a toothpick inserted in center comes out clean. Place baking dish on a wire rack and let set for at least 15 minutes. Cut into 8 servings.

Each serving equals:

HE: 1 Bread • 1 Fruit • 16 Optional Calories

142 Calories • 2 gm Fat • 3 gm Protein •
28 gm Carbohydrate • 303 mg Sodium •
26 mg Calcium • 0 gm Fiber

DIABETIC: 1 Starch • 1 Fruit

Country Lane Apple Coffeecake

What a luscious combination apples and maple syrup make in this biscuit-based coffeecake that's amazingly sweet! Don't be surprised if everyone wants to lick the pan once you finish serving this tempting treat. ☻ Serves 6

1½ cups cored, peeled, and finely chopped cooking apples ☆
1 (7.5-ounce) can Pillsbury refrigerated buttermilk biscuits
½ cup Cary's Sugar Free Maple Syrup
½ teaspoon apple pie spice
2 tablespoons pourable Sugar Twin
1 egg or equivalent in egg substitute
¼ cup (1 ounce) chopped walnuts

Preheat oven to 375 degrees. Spray a 9-inch pie plate with butter-flavored cooking spray. Evenly sprinkle 1 cup apples into prepared pie plate. Separate biscuits and cut each into 4 pieces. Evenly sprinkle biscuit pieces over apples. Top with remaining ½ cup apples. In a small bowl, combine maple syrup, apple pie spice, Sugar Twin, and egg. Stir in walnuts. Spoon syrup mixture evenly over top. Bake for 35 to 45 minutes. Place pie plate on a wire rack and let set for at least 5 minutes. Cut into 6 wedges.

Each serving equals:

HE: 1¼ Bread • ½ Fruit • ⅓ Protein • ⅓ Fat •
15 Optional Calories

---

161 Calories • 5 gm Fat • 4 gm Protein •
25 gm Carbohydrate • 360 mg Sodium •
11 mg Calcium • 2 gm Fiber

DIABETIC: 1 Starch • ½ Fruit • ½ Fat

Pear-Walnut Coffeecake

Here's another one of what I call my "pantry pleasers"—a fruity dessert that can be prepared with ease from ingredients you keep on hand, and that doesn't require fresh fruit in season. Haven't you loved the delicate flavor and luscious texture of canned pears since childhood? ☺ Serves 8

1½ cups Bisquick Reduced Fat Baking Mix
⅓ cup pourable Sugar Twin
1 teaspoon apple pie spice
¼ cup (1 ounce) chopped walnuts
2 cups (one 16-ounce can) pears, packed in fruit juice, drained
    and chopped, and ½ cup liquid reserved
1 egg or equivalent in egg substitute
⅓ cup Land O Lakes no-fat sour cream

Preheat oven to 375 degrees. Spray an 8-by-8-inch baking dish with butter-flavored cooking spray. In a large bowl, combine baking mix, Sugar Twin, apple pie spice, and walnuts. Stir in pears. Add reserved pear liquid, egg, and sour cream. Mix gently just to combine. Evenly spread batter into prepared baking dish. Bake for 25 to 35 minutes or until a toothpick inserted in center comes out clean. Place baking dish on a wire rack and let set for at least 15 minutes. Cut into 8 servings.

Each serving equals:

HE: 1 Bread • ½ Fruit • ¼ Protein • ¼ Fat •
14 Optional Calories

160 Calories • 4 gm Fat • 3 gm Protein •
28 gm Carbohydrate • 286 mg Sodium •
38 mg Calcium • 2 gm Fiber

DIABETIC: 1 Starch • ½ Fruit • ½ Fat

Orange-Nutmeg Coffeecake

Nutmeg is often overshadowed by cinnamon when it comes to baking, but it has a unique flavor all its own. Here, it gives a plain orange coffeecake some special pizzazz! ♥ Serves 8

1½ cups Bisquick Reduced Fat Baking Mix
2 tablespoons pourable Sugar Twin
½ teaspoon ground nutmeg
¼ cup (1 ounce) chopped pecans
¼ cup Land O Lakes no-fat sour cream
½ cup skim milk
½ cup orange marmalade spreadable fruit

Preheat oven to 375 degrees. Spray an 8-by-8-inch baking dish with butter-flavored cooking spray. In a large bowl, combine baking mix, Sugar Twin, nutmeg, and pecans. Add sour cream and skim milk. Mix well to combine. Evenly spread half of batter into prepared baking dish. Drop spreadable fruit by spoonfuls evenly over batter. Evenly spread remaining batter over top. Bake for 20 to 30 minutes or until a toothpick inserted in center comes out clean. Place baking dish on a wire rack and let set for at least 15 minutes. Cut into 8 servings.

Each serving equals:

HE: 1 Bread • 1 Fruit • ½ Fat • 15 Optional Calories

160 Calories • 4 gm Fat • 3 gm Protein •
28 gm Carbohydrate • 279 mg Sodium •
47 mg Calcium • 0 gm Fiber

DIABETIC: 1 Starch • 1 Fruit • ½ Fat

Choco-Coconut Isle Orange Coffeecake

This pleases my grandson Zach so much when I get up early to bake it for him! He adores the coconut combined with the mini chips, and he smiles when I pour orange juice into the batter. (He has the greatest smile!)   ☻   Serves 8

> 1½ cups Bisquick Reduced Fat Baking Mix
> ⅔ cup Carnation Nonfat Dry Milk Powder
> ½ cup pourable Sugar Twin
> 1 cup unsweetened orange juice
> ¼ cup Land O Lakes no-fat sour cream
> 1 teaspoon coconut extract
> ¼ cup (1 ounce) mini chocolate chips
> 2 tablespoons flaked coconut

Preheat oven to 375 degrees. Spray an 8-by-8-inch baking dish with butter-flavored cooking spray. In a large bowl, combine baking mix, dry milk powder, and Sugar Twin. Add orange juice, sour cream, and coconut extract. Mix gently just to combine. Fold in chocolate chips. Evenly spread batter into prepared baking dish. Sprinkle coconut evenly over top. Bake for 25 to 35 minutes or until a toothpick inserted in center comes out clean. Place baking dish on a wire rack and let set for at least 15 minutes. Cut into 8 servings.

Each serving equals:

HE: 1 Bread • ¼ Skim Milk • ¼ Fruit • ¼ Slider • 16 Optional Calories

147 Calories • 3 gm Fat • 4 gm Protein • 26 gm Carbohydrate • 306 mg Sodium • 99 mg Calcium • 1 gm Fiber

DIABETIC: 1½ Starch/Carbohydrate • ½ Fat

Applesauce-Raisin Coffeecake

Talk about temptation-on-a-plate! This is one of the richest-tasting coffeecakes in the entire book, because it's got a dough made even more delectable by the addition of fat-free cream cheese. You could save this for a special occasion—or make it tonight!

❍ Serves 8

> 1½ cups Bisquick Reduced Fat Baking Mix
> 1 (4-serving) package JELL-O sugar-free instant vanilla pudding mix
> 1½ teaspoons apple pie spice
> ½ cup + 2 tablespoons raisins
> 1½ cups unsweetened applesauce
> 1 (8-ounce) package Philadelphia fat-free cream cheese
> 1 teaspoon vanilla extract
> Sugar substitute to equal ¼ cup sugar
> 2 tablespoons (½ ounce) chopped walnuts

Preheat oven to 375 degrees. Spray an 8-by-8-inch baking dish with butter-flavored cooking spray. In a large bowl, combine baking mix, dry pudding mix, apple pie spice, and raisins. Add applesauce. Mix well to combine. Evenly spread batter into prepared baking dish. Bake for 35 to 45 minutes or until a toothpick inserted in center comes out clean. Place baking dish on a wire rack and allow to cool. In a small bowl, stir cream cheese with a spoon until soft. Stir in vanilla extract and sugar substitute. Spread topping mixture evenly over cooled coffeecake. Sprinkle walnuts evenly over top. Cut into 8 servings.

Each serving equals:

> HE: 1 Bread • 1 Fruit • ½ Protein • ¼ Slider •
> 5 Optional Calories
> _____
> 183 Calories • 3 gm Fat • 6 gm Protein •
> 33 gm Carbohydrate • 598 mg Sodium •
> 26 mg Calcium • 1 gm Fiber
> _____
> DIABETIC: 1 Starch • 1 Fruit • ½ Meat

Apple Harvest Coffeecake

If you weren't raised by a mother or grandmother who baked, then you might not be sure what the difference is between a cooking apple and an eating apple. Eating apples taste best raw, like Red or Golden Delicious. Cooking apples (Macintosh or Granny Smith) are firm and flavorful enough to stand up to baking.

● Serves 8

> 1½ cups all-purpose flour
> 1 (4-serving) package JELL-O sugar-free instant vanilla pudding mix
> 1 teaspoon baking powder
> ½ teaspoon baking soda
> ⅔ cup Carnation Nonfat Dry Milk Powder
> ¾ cup water
> 1 egg or equivalent in egg substitute
> ⅓ cup unsweetened applesauce
> 1 cup (2 small) cored, unpeeled, and sliced cooking apples
> ½ teaspoon ground cinnamon
> 2 tablespoons pourable Sugar Twin

Preheat oven to 375 degrees. Spray an 8-by-8-inch baking dish with butter-flavored cooking spray. In a large bowl, combine flour, dry pudding mix, baking powder, and baking soda. In a small bowl, combine dry milk powder and water. Stir in egg and applesauce. Add milk mixture to flour mixture. Mix gently just to combine. Evenly spread batter into prepared baking dish. Place sliced apples over top. In another small bowl, combine cinnamon and Sugar Twin. Sprinkle cinnamon mixture evenly over apples. Lightly spray top with butter-flavored cooking spray. Bake for 35 to 40 minutes or until a toothpick inserted in center comes out clean. Place baking dish on a wire rack and let set for at least 15 minutes. Cut into 8 servings.

HINT: Also good with 2 tablespoons walnuts stirred into batter.

Each serving equals:

HE: 1 Bread • ⅓ Fruit • ¼ Skim Milk • ¼ Slider • 2 Optional Calories

---

137 Calories • 1 gm Fat • 5 gm Protein • 27 gm Carbohydrate • 344 mg Sodium • 112 mg Calcium • 1 gm Fiber

---

DIABETIC: 2 Starch

Berry Delicious Coffeecake

One of the ways I like to show my love for people is by creating recipes featuring the flavors they like best. Well, this one was invented with me in mind! My strawberry patches have to work extra hard to keep me in my favorite berries.   ●   Serves 8

> 1½ cups Bisquick Reduced Fat Baking Mix
> ½ cup pourable Sugar Twin
> ½ teaspoon ground cinnamon
> ¼ cup (1 ounce) chopped walnuts
> ½ cup unsweetened applesauce
> 1 egg or equivalent in egg substitute
> 2 tablespoons Land O Lakes no-fat sour cream
> 1 cup finely chopped fresh strawberries

Preheat oven to 375 degrees. Spray an 8-by-8-inch baking dish with butter-flavored cooking spray. In a large bowl, combine baking mix, Sugar Twin, cinnamon, and walnuts. In a small bowl, combine applesauce, egg, and sour cream. Add applesauce mixture to baking mix mixture. Mix well to combine. Fold in strawberries. Evenly spread batter into prepared baking dish. Bake for 20 to 30 minutes or until a toothpick inserted in center comes out clean. Place baking dish on a wire rack and let set for at least 15 minutes. Cut into 8 servings.

Each serving equals:

HE: 1 Bread • ¼ Protein • ¼ Fruit • ¼ Fat • 10 Optional Calories

---

128 Calories • 4 gm Fat • 3 gm Protein • 20 gm Carbohydrate • 275 mg Sodium • 33 mg Calcium • 1 gm Fiber

---

DIABETIC: 1½ Starch/Carbohydrate • ½ Fat

The Variety Bread Basket

No matter where you are, Sunday dinner always begins with the arrival of the bread basket—and I can almost hear those rumbling tummies start to quiet down as everyone at the table tucks into one of my old-fashioned rolls or biscuits. It's a moment in which every restaurant can win or lose a customer forever. No matter where you're eating, you await the arrival of the bread with interest—and when you begin to look through the basket and make your choice, you know right then how much you're going to enjoy your meal!

If you're used to warming up and serving just one kind of bread at your house, maybe it's time to spread your wings and surprise the diners gathered around your table. I'm not suggesting you give up all your hobbies to begin baking round the clock, but I believe you'll have a good time choosing a few recipes from this section to vary the choices you offer your guests.

This section provides just what it promises—a mélange of baked delights to serve for all kinds of occasions, or even just to please yourself! How about inviting friends for an afternoon tea party and offering **Apricot Coconut Kolaches** and **Fast Fruit Focaccia**? Instead of tearing open bags of chips for a family afternoon in front of the TV, you could raise more cheers than the home team by passing a tray of **Cheesy Garlic Biscuits** and **Olé Cheese Twists.** I'd be glad to wake up to a birthday party brunch that featured **Gooey Cinnamon Rolls** and **Apple Flat Biscuits**, wouldn't you? Yum!

The Variety Bread Basket

Marmalade Sunrise Rolls

Sure, a little spreadable fruit on a piece of toast is probably "good enough" for most people for a quickie breakfast. But why settle for "good enough" when these sunny and speedy treats take very little effort—and look and taste really special!   ☺   Serves 8

1½ cups Bisquick Reduced Fat Baking Mix
2 tablespoons pourable Sugar Twin
2 tablespoons Land O Lakes no-fat sour cream
⅓ cup skim milk
6 tablespoons orange marmalade spreadable fruit

Preheat oven to 415 degrees. Spray a large baking sheet with butter-flavored cooking spray. In a large bowl, combine baking mix, Sugar Twin, sour cream, and skim milk. Mix gently until mixture forms a soft dough. Gently knead in bowl 8 to 10 times. Place dough between 2 large sheets of waxed paper and roll into an 8-by-12-inch rectangle. Lightly spray dough with butter-flavored cooking spray. Evenly spread orange marmalade over top. Roll up jelly-roll style and seal edges. Cut into 8 rolls. Arrange rolls on prepared baking sheet. Lightly spray tops with butter-flavored cooking spray. Bake for 8 to 10 minutes or until golden brown. Serve warm.

Hints: 1. Spreadable fruit spreads best at room temperature.
2. Use any flavor spreadable fruit of your choice.

Each serving equals:

HE: 1 Bread • ¾ Fruit • 9 Optional Calories

---

121 Calories • 1 gm Fat • 2 gm Protein •
26 gm Carbohydrate • 272 mg Sodium •
35 mg Calcium • 0 gm Fiber

DIABETIC: 1 Starch • 1 Fruit

Blueberry-Orange Breakfast Biscuits

Fresh biscuits studded with plump blueberries—and ready in just 15 minutes? If that's not a recipe for morning magic, I don't know what is! Tuck these into the oven, take a quick shower, and before you know it, breakfast is ready!   ☻   Serves 8

> 1½ cups Bisquick Reduced Fat Baking Mix
> ½ cup pourable Sugar Twin
> ¾ cup fresh blueberries
> ½ cup unsweetened orange juice
> 2 tablespoons Kraft fat-free mayonnaise

Preheat oven to 425 degrees. Spray a large baking sheet with butter-flavored cooking spray. In a large bowl, combine baking mix, Sugar Twin, and blueberries. In a medium bowl, combine orange juice and mayonnaise. Add orange juice mixture to baking mix mixture. Mix gently just to combine. Drop by tablespoonful onto prepared baking sheet to form 8 biscuits. Bake for 8 to 12 minutes or until golden brown. Place baking sheet on a wire rack and let set for 2 to 3 minutes. Serve warm.

Each serving equals:

HE: 1 Bread • ¼ Fruit • 9 Optional Calories

97 Calories • 1 gm Fat • 2 gm Protein •
20 gm Carbohydrate • 295 mg Sodium •
20 mg Calcium • 1 gm Fiber

DIABETIC: 1½ Starch/Carbohydrate

Apple Flat Biscuits

No, I didn't create this recipe because my box of Wheat Chex got squashed in the trunk of the car! But adding some tasty texture to these sweet-and-tart breakfast beauties gives them extra-special goodness.   ☻   Serves 8

> ⅓ cup (1½ ounces) crushed Wheat Chex
>
> 1 cup + 2 tablespoons Bisquick Reduced Fat Baking Mix
>
> 2 tablespoons pourable Sugar Twin
>
> ½ teaspoon apple pie spice
>
> ½ cup (1 small) cored, unpeeled, and finely chopped cooking apple
>
> ½ cup unsweetened apple juice

Preheat oven to 450 degrees. Spray a large baking sheet with butter-flavored cooking spray. In a large bowl, combine crushed Wheat Chex, baking mix, Sugar Twin, and apple pie spice. Add apple and apple juice. Mix gently just to combine. Drop by tablespoonful onto prepared baking sheet to form 8 biscuits. Bake for 8 to 10 minutes. Place baking sheet on a wire rack and let set for at least 5 minutes.

Hints: 1. A self-seal sandwich bag works great for crushing Wheat Chex.
2. Biscuits will flatten naturally when baking and will resemble cookies.
3. Good served warm with apple butter.

Each serving equals:

HE: 1 Bread • ¼ Fruit • 1 Optional Calorie

93 Calories • 1 gm Fat • 2 gm Protein • 19 gm Carbohydrate • 232 mg Sodium • 17 mg Calcium • 1 gm Fiber

DIABETIC: 1 Starch

Festive Drop Biscuits

These look pretty enough for a party, so you might want to put them on the menu when you're having company for brunch. If you've never used rum extract, and you're not sure if you'll like the taste, start with a half teaspoon the first time you prepare these.

◑ Serves 8

> 1½ cups Bisquick Reduced Fat Baking Mix
> 1 cup raisins
> ¼ cup (1 ounce) chopped pecans
> ½ cup skim milk
> 1 teaspoon rum extract
> 8 maraschino cherries, quartered

Preheat oven to 375 degrees. Spray a large baking sheet with butter-flavored cooking spray. In a large bowl, combine baking mix, raisins, and pecans. Add skim milk and rum extract. Mix gently to combine. Fold in cherry pieces. Drop by tablespoonful onto prepared baking sheet to form 8 biscuits. Bake for 18 to 22 minutes or until tops are lightly browned. Lightly spray tops with butter-flavored cooking spray. Place baking sheet on a wire rack and let set for at least 5 minutes.

Each serving equals:

HE: 1 Bread • 1 Fruit • ½ Fat • 16 Optional Calories

184 Calories • 4 gm Fat • 3 gm Protein •
34 gm Carbohydrate • 271 mg Sodium •
47 mg Calcium • 1 gm Fiber

DIABETIC: 1 Starch • 1 Fruit • ½ Fat

Hawaiian Sugar Snacks

You want your family to eat healthy, even when they're nibbling between meals. Here's a real tummy-pleaser that will appeal to young and old alike. They're oh-so-sweet and wonderfully moist—perfect for gobbling when the "hungries" hit!

❂ Serves 8

> 1 cup (one 8-ounce can) crushed pineapple, packed in fruit juice, drained, and ¼ cup liquid reserved
> ¼ cup Land O Lakes no-fat sour cream
> ¼ cup + 2 tablespoons pourable Sugar Twin ☆
> 2 tablespoons Brown Sugar Twin
> ½ teaspoon apple pie spice
> ¼ cup skim milk
> 1½ cups Bisquick Reduced Fat baking mix

Preheat oven to 415 degrees. Spray 8 wells of a 12-hole muffin pan with butter-flavored cooking spray or line with paper liners. In a large bowl, combine pineapple, sour cream, ¼ cup Sugar Twin, Brown Sugar Twin, and apple pie spice. Stir in reserved pineapple liquid and skim milk. Add baking mix. Mix gently to combine. Evenly spoon batter into prepared muffin wells. Sprinkle about ¾ teaspoon Sugar Twin over top of each. Bake for 15 to 20 minutes. Place muffin pan on a wire rack and let set for 5 minutes. Remove buns from pan and continue cooling on wire rack.

Each serving equals:

HE: 1 Bread • ¼ Fruit • 16 Optional Calories
___
105 Calories • 1 gm Fat • 2 gm Protein •
22 gm Carbohydrate • 276 mg Sodium •
40 mg Calcium • 1 gm Fiber
___
DIABETIC: 1½ Starch/Carbohydrate

Cinnamon Twists

We made lots of these when we were testing the recipe, and they all disappeared! *Hmm,* what can that mean? I guess they're as delectable and fun to eat as I hoped they'd be!

◑ Serves 5 (2 each)

> 1 (7.5-ounce) can Pillsbury refrigerated buttermilk biscuits
> ½ cup pourable Sugar Twin
> 2 teaspoons ground cinnamon

Preheat oven to 425 degrees. Spray a large baking sheet with butter-flavored cooking spray. Separate biscuits. Roll each biscuit into a 9-inch rope. Bring the ends of each together and pinch to seal. In a saucer, combine Sugar Twin and cinnamon. Lightly spray each biscuit rope with butter-flavored cooking spray and dip in cinnamon mixture. Twist each into a figure eight. Place on prepared baking sheet. Spray tops with butter-flavored cooking spray. Bake for 5 to 6 minutes. Serve warm.

HINT: Roll each biscuit between your hands (which have been sprayed with a little cooking spray) until you get to the 9 inches.

Each serving equals:

HE: 1½ Bread • 10 Optional Calories

105 Calories • 1 gm Fat • 3 gm Protein •
21 gm Carbohydrate • 365 mg Sodium •
11 mg Calcium • 3 gm Fiber

DIABETIC: 1½ Starch

Gooey Cinnamon Rolls

There's something intoxicating about the huge and luscious cinnamon rolls sold in malls across the country, but those tend to be high in calories, sugar, and fat. Still, why should you be deprived of such a delightful temptation? Here's my Healthy Exchanges version for you to enjoy whenever you like!

⊘ Serves 5 (2 each)

> 1 (7.5-ounce) can Pillsbury refrigerated buttermilk biscuits
> ¼ cup pourable Sugar Twin
> 1½ teaspoons ground cinnamon
> ½ cup (1 ounce) miniature marshmallows

Preheat oven to 400 degrees. Spray 10 wells of a 12-hole muffin pan with butter-flavored cooking spray. Separate biscuits. Flatten each into a 4-inch circle. In a small bowl, combine Sugar Twin and cinnamon. Dip each biscuit into cinnamon mixture. Place about 4 mini marshmallows in center of each biscuit. Bring edges up to form balls. Place each in a prepared muffin well, seam side down. Bake for 8 to 10 minutes. Remove rolls from pan immediately and cool slightly on a wire rack.

Each serving equals:

HE: 1½ Bread • 15 Optional Calories

---

117 Calories • 1 gm Fat • 3 gm Protein •
24 gm Carbohydrate • 367 mg Sodium •
8 mg Calcium • 2 gm Fiber

DIABETIC: 1½ Starch/Carbohydrate

Biscuit Cinnamon Rolls

It's a biscuit! It's a cinnamon roll! Why, it's both—how did I do that? When you use the best possible prepared foods, you can learn to work real culinary magic in very little time.

○ Serves 5 (2 each)

> ½ cup Brown Sugar Twin ☆
> 1 (7.5-ounce) can Pillsbury refrigerated buttermilk biscuits
> 2½ teaspoons ground cinnamon
> 5 tablespoons raisins

Preheat oven to 350 degrees. Spray 10 wells of a 12-hole muffin pan with butter-flavored cooking spray. Sprinkle ½ teaspoon Brown Sugar Twin into prepared muffin wells. Separate biscuits and press each into a rectangular shape. Spray each with butter-flavored cooking spray. Sprinkle 2 teaspoons Brown Sugar Twin, ¼ teaspoon cinnamon, and ½ tablespoon raisins on each biscuit. Roll each up lengthwise, pinching edges together. Cut each roll into 3 pieces and arrange cloverleaf fashion in muffin cups. Lightly spray tops with butter-flavored cooking spray. Bake for 10 to 12 minutes. Place muffin pan on a wire rack and let set for 5 minutes. Serve warm.

Each serving equals:

HE: 1½ Bread • ½ Fruit • 8 Optional Calories

---

128 Calories • 0 gm Fat • 4 gm Protein • 28 gm Carbohydrate • 183 mg Sodium • 9 mg Calcium • 1 gm Fiber

---

DIABETIC: 1½ Starch

Apricot Tea Flatbread

Company just walked in the door, and you've got to come up with something quick? This will polish your star as an instant chef! Serve these up only minutes after guests arrive, and you're sure to win applause.   ◐   Serves 5 (2 each)

> 1 (7.5-ounce) can Pillsbury refrigerated buttermilk biscuits
> 3 tablespoons + 1 teaspoon apricot spreadable fruit
> 2 tablespoons pourable Sugar Twin
> ½ teaspoon ground cinnamon

Preheat oven to 425 degrees. Separate biscuits. Flatten each and place on a large ungreased baking sheet. Lightly spray tops with butter-flavored cooking spray. Spread 1 teaspoon spreadable fruit over each. In a small bowl, combine Sugar Twin and cinnamon. Sprinkle mixture evenly over tops. Bake for 5 minutes. Place baking sheet on a wire rack and let set for 2 to 3 minutes. Serve warm.

HINT: Spreadable fruit spreads best at room temperature.

Each serving equals:

HE: 1½ Bread • ⅔ Fruit • 2 Optional Calories

---

129 Calories • 1 gm Fat • 3 gm Protein •
27 gm Carbohydrate • 365 mg Sodium •
3 mg Calcium • 2 gm Fiber

DIABETIC: 1½ Starch

Chocolate-Strawberry Turnovers

Here's a fun recipe to serve when your children are having friends over. It's so simple, they can help spread the filling and place the chocolate chips. When they're a bit older, they can use the tines of a fork to seal the little pastries. ❂ Serves 5 (2 each)

> 1 (7.5-ounce) can Pillsbury refrigerated biscuits
> 5 teaspoons strawberry spreadable fruit
> 1 tablespoon (¼ ounce) mini chocolate chips
> 1 teaspoon pourable Sugar Twin

Preheat oven to 425 degrees. Spray a baking sheet with butter-flavored cooking spray. Separate and place biscuits on prepared baking sheet. Flatten each biscuit into a 4-inch circle. Spread ½ teaspoon spreadable fruit on half of each biscuit and sprinkle a full ¼ teaspoon chocolate chips over top. Fold each biscuit in half and seal edges with a fork. Lightly spray tops with butter-flavored cooking spray. Sprinkle Sugar Twin evenly over tops. Bake for 7 to 8 minutes or until golden brown. Place baking sheet on a wire rack and let set for 2 to 3 minutes. Serve warm.

Hints: 1. Be sure to seal edges well with fork or fruit will bake out.
  2. Freeze leftovers and reheat in microwave.

Each serving equals:

HE: 1½ Bread • ⅓ Fruit • 8 Optional Calories

126 Calories • 2 gm Fat • 3 gm Protein • 24 gm Carbohydrate • 365 mg Sodium • 0 mg Calcium • 2 gm Fiber

DIABETIC: 2 Starch • ½ Fat

Fast Fruit Focaccia

Most focaccia recipes are savory, not sweet, but I thought the same tasty principle would apply if you wanted to feature fruit and nuts instead of spiced veggies on top!   ☺   Serves 6

> ¼ cup pourable Sugar Twin
> 1 (7.5-ounce) can Pillsbury refrigerated buttermilk biscuits
> 1 cup (one 8-ounce can) fruit cocktail, packed in fruit juice,
>   drained
> 2 tablespoons (½ ounce) chopped pecans
> 2 tablespoons apricot spreadable fruit

Preheat oven to 375 degrees. Spray a 9-inch pie plate with butter-flavored cooking spray. Place Sugar Twin in a small bowl. Separate biscuits and roll each in Sugar Twin. Pat biscuits into prepared pie plate. Evenly sprinkle fruit cocktail and pecans over biscuits. Place spreadable fruit in a 1-cup glass measuring cup. Microwave on HIGH (100% power) for 15 to 20 seconds. Drizzle melted spreadable fruit over fruit cocktail. Bake for 25 minutes. Place pie plate on a wire rack and let set for at least 5 minutes. Cut into 6 wedges.

Each serving equals:

HE: 1¼ Bread • ⅔ Fruit • ⅓ Fat •
4 Optional Calories

---

130 Calories • 2 gm Fat • 3 gm Protein •
25 gm Carbohydrate • 305 mg Sodium •
4 mg Calcium • 2 gm Fiber

DIABETIC: 1 Starch • ½ Fat

Apricot-Coconut Kolaches

If you've ever tasted my cherry kolaches, the fruit-topped rolls we serve in JO's Kitchen Cafe, then you'll want to try this variation. With just one bite, you'll be transported to the tropics without a passport or a plane ticket! ☻ Serves 12

> 12 Rhodes frozen yeast dinner rolls
> 2 cups (9 ounces) finely chopped dried apricots
> ¼ cup Brown Sugar Twin
> 2 teaspoons coconut extract
> 2 tablespoons unsweetened applesauce
> 2 tablespoons flaked coconut

Spray a large baking sheet with butter-flavored cooking spray. Evenly space frozen rolls on prepared sheet. Cover with cloth and let rolls thaw and rise. After rolls have risen, place apricots in a medium bowl and cover with 1 cup boiling water. Let set for 5 minutes. Drain and return softened apricots to bowl. Add Brown Sugar Twin, coconut extract, and applesauce. Mix gently to combine. Make an indentation in center of each roll. Evenly fill indentations with a full tablespoon of apricot mixture. Sprinkle ½ teaspoon coconut over top of each. Cover with cloth again and let rolls rest for 10 minutes. Lightly spray top of each roll with butter-flavored cooking spray. Bake for 10 to 15 minutes at 400 degrees or until golden brown. Lightly spray tops again with butter-flavored cooking spray. Place baking sheet on a wire rack and let set for 5 minutes. Remove rolls and continue cooling on wire rack.

Each serving equals:

HE: 1 Bread • 1 Fruit • 5 Optional Calories

162 Calories • 2 gm Fat • 5 gm Protein •
31 gm Carbohydrate • 275 mg Sodium •
10 mg Calcium • 4 gm Fiber

DIABETIC: 1 Starch • 1 Fruit

Paradise Fruit Rolls

Here's my version of a healthy "cheese Danish" that is so fruity and rich, so creamy and nutty, you'll never settle for the store-bought kind again! I prefer this with apricot spreadable fruit, but if you're a fan of raspberry give it a try instead,　　　○　　Serves 12

12 Rhodes frozen yeast dinner rolls

¾ cup (6 ounces) Philadelphia fat-free cream cheese

1 tablespoon Brown Sugar Twin

1 tablespoon apricot spreadable fruit

1 cup (one 8-ounce can) crushed pineapple, packed in fruit juice, well drained

3 tablespoons (¾ ounce) chopped pecans

Spray a large baking sheet with butter-flavored cooking spray. Evenly space frozen rolls on prepared sheet. Cover with cloth and let rolls thaw and rise. Make an indentation in center of each roll. In a medium bowl, stir cream cheese with a spoon until soft. Blend in Brown Sugar Twin and spreadable fruit. Add pineapple and pecans. Mix gently to combine. Evenly fill indentations with a full tablespoon of cream cheese mixture. Cover with cloth again and let rolls rest for 10 minutes. Lightly spray top of each roll with butter-flavored cooking spray. Bake for 10 to 15 minutes at 400 degrees or until rolls are golden brown. Lightly spray tops again with butter-flavored cooking spray. Place baking sheet on a wire rack and let set for 5 minutes. Remove rolls and continue cooling on wire rack.

HINT:　Refrigerate leftovers and re-warm in microwave.

Each serving equals:

HE: 1 Bread • ¼ Protein • ¼ Fruit • ¼ Fat •
1 Optional Calorie

143 Calories • 3 gm Fat • 6 gm Protein •
23 gm Carbohydrate • 355 mg Sodium •
4 mg Calcium • 1 gm Fiber

DIABETIC: 1 Starch • ½ Fruit

Brunch Pineapple Pecan Rolls

So much pleasure in every bite of these pecan-studded delights! They're terrific served warm or cold, so see what you prefer!

● Serves 8

> 8 Rhodes frozen yeast dinner rolls
> 1 (4-serving) package JELL-O sugar-free vanilla cook-and-serve pudding mix
> 1 (4-serving) package JELL-O sugar-free lemon gelatin
> 1 cup (one 8-ounce can) crushed pineapple, packed in fruit juice, undrained
> ¾ cup water
> ¼ cup (1 ounce) chopped pecans

Place rolls in a 9-by-9-inch cake pan sprayed with butter-flavored cooking spray. Cover with cloth and let rolls thaw and rise. In a medium saucepan, combine dry pudding mix and dry gelatin. Add undrained pineapple and water. Mix well to combine. Cook over medium heat until mixture thickens and starts to boil, stirring often. Remove from heat. Stir in pecans. Place saucepan on a wire rack and let cool completely until rolls have risen. Spoon cooled pineapple mixture evenly over rolls. Let set for 10 minutes. Bake at 375 degrees for 15 to 20 minutes. Place cake pan on a wire rack and let set for at least 15 minutes. Divide into 8 servings.

Each serving equals:

HE: 1 Bread • ½ Fat • ¼ Fruit • 15 Optional Calories

160 Calories • 4 gm Fat • 5 gm Protein •
26 gm Carbohydrate • 355 mg Sodium •
6 mg Calcium • 1 gm Fiber

DIABETIC: 1½ Starch/Carbohydrate • ½ Fat

Maple "Sugar" Buns

Some people refer to these nutty-sweet treasures as sticky buns, but whatever you call them, you'll soon decide they're a temptation too delicious to resist! ☻ Serves 12

1 tablespoon Cary's Sugar Free Maple Syrup
½ cup Brown Sugar Twin
¼ cup reduced-calorie margarine
⅓ cup (1½ ounces) chopped pecans
12 Rhodes frozen yeast dinner rolls

In a medium saucepan, combine maple syrup, Brown Sugar Twin, and margarine. Cook over medium heat until mixture starts to boil, stirring often. Remove from heat. Stir in pecans. Evenly divide mixture among the wells of a 12-hole muffin pan. Place 1 frozen roll over top of each. Lightly spray tops with butter-flavored cooking spray. Cover with a cloth and let thaw and rise. Bake at 375 degrees for 15 minutes. Lightly spray tops again with butter-flavored cooking spray. Remove buns from pan and cool on a wire rack.

Each serving equals:

HE: 1 Bread • 1 Fat • 5 Optional Calories

142 Calories • 6 gm Fat • 4 gm Protein •
18 gm Carbohydrate • 291 mg Sodium •
1 mg Calcium • 1 gm Fiber

DIABETIC: 1 Starch • 1 Fat

Blueberry-Peach Fruit Treats

This delectable dessert looks magnificent when you bring it to the table, with so much colorful fruit piled on top of the crust! It's great for a family reunion or special anniversary party, when you want everything to look as festive as possible—and taste scrumptious!

○ Serves 12

1 (8-ounce) can Pillsbury Reduced Fat Crescent Rolls
1 (8-ounce) package Philadelphia fat-free cream cheese
Sugar substitute to equal 2 tablespoons sugar
1 teaspoon vanilla extract
1 cup (one 8-ounce can) crushed pineapple, packed in fruit juice,
    drained, and ¼ cup liquid reserved
2 cups (one 16-ounce can) sliced peaches, packed in fruit juice,
    drained and coarsely chopped, and ½ cup liquid reserved
1½ cups fresh or frozen blueberries, thawed and drained
¾ cup water
1 (4-serving) package JELL-O sugar-free vanilla cook-and-serve
    pudding mix
1 (4-serving) package JELL-O sugar-free lemon gelatin
¼ teaspoon ground nutmeg

Preheat oven to 415 degrees. Spray a rimmed 10-by-15-inch baking sheet with butter-flavored cooking spray. Unroll crescent rolls and pat into sheet, being sure to seal perforations. Bake for 6 to 7 minutes or until light golden brown. Place baking sheet on a wire rack and allow to cool. Meanwhile, in a medium bowl, stir cream cheese with a spoon until soft. Add sugar substitute and vanilla extract. Blend in pineapple. Evenly spread mixture over cooled crust. Evenly sprinkle peaches and blueberries over cream cheese mixture. In a medium saucepan, combine reserved pineapple liquid, peach liquid, and water. Add dry pudding mix, dry gelatin, and nutmeg. Mix well to combine. Cook over medium heat until mixture thickens and starts to boil, stirring constantly. Evenly spoon hot mixture over fruit. Refrigerate for at least 1 hour. Cut into 12 servings.

Each serving equals:

HE: ⅔ Bread • ⅔ Fruit • ⅓ Protein •
11 Optional Calories

131 Calories • 3 gm Fat • 5 gm Protein •
21 gm Carbohydrate • 328 mg Sodium •
7 mg Calcium • 1 gm Fiber

DIABETIC: 1 Fruit • ½ Starch • ½ Meat

Cheesy Garlic Biscuits

Here's a super savory delight that just doesn't look or taste "healthy"! Served up golden brown and fragrant with rich flavor, these will get every appetite primed for a delicious dinner.

● Serves 4

¾ cup Bisquick Reduced Fat Baking Mix
⅓ cup Carnation Nonfat Dry Milk Powder
2 tablespoons pourable Sugar Twin
¼ teaspoon dried minced garlic
¼ cup (¾ ounce) grated Kraft reduced-fat American cheese
2 tablespoons Kraft fat-free mayonnaise
¼ cup water

Preheat oven to 415 degrees. Spray a baking sheet with butter-flavored cooking spray. In a medium bowl, combine baking mix, dry milk powder, and Sugar Twin. Stir in garlic and American cheese. Add mayonnaise and water. Mix well to combine. Drop by tablespoonful onto prepared baking sheet to form 4 biscuits. Bake for 8 to 12 minutes or until golden brown. Remove from oven. Lightly spray tops with butter-flavored cooking spray. Place baking sheet on a wire rack and let set for at least 5 minutes. Serve warm.

Each serving equals:

HE: 1 Bread • ¼ Skim Milk • ¼ Protein •
8 Optional Calories

122 Calories • 2 gm Fat • 5 gm Protein •
21 gm Carbohydrate • 441 mg Sodium •
118 mg Calcium • 0 gm Fiber

DIABETIC: 1½ Starch/Carbohydrate

Zucchini-Onion Biscuits

What an amazing aroma these delectable biscuits provide when you fold back the pretty napkin covering your bread basket! See if that luscious cheese and tangy seasoning are enough to make your family cheer! ◑ Serves 8 (2 each)

1½ cups all-purpose flour
½ cup finely chopped onion
¼ cup (¾ ounce) grated Kraft fat-free Parmesan cheese
2 teaspoons baking powder
½ teaspoon baking soda
1 teaspoon Italian seasoning
⅔ cup Carnation Nonfat Dry Milk Powder
½ cup water
1½ teaspoons white vinegar
1 egg or equivalent in egg substitute
½ cup shredded unpeeled zucchini

Preheat oven to 375 degrees. Spray a baking sheet with butter-flavored cooking spray. In a large bowl, combine flour, onion, Parmesan cheese, baking powder, baking soda, and Italian seasoning. In a small bowl, combine dry milk powder, water, and vinegar. Add egg. Mix well to combine. Stir in zucchini. Add milk mixture to flour mixture. Mix just until blended. Drop by tablespoonful onto prepared baking sheet to form 16 biscuits. Bake for 8 to 12 minutes or until lightly browned. Lightly spray tops with butter-flavored cooking spray. Serve warm.

Each serving equals:

HE: 1 Bread • ¼ Skim Milk • ¼ Protein •
¼ Vegetable

125 Calories • 1 gm Fat • 5 gm Protein •
24 gm Carbohydrate • 287 mg Sodium •
146 mg Calcium • 1 gm Fiber

DIABETIC: 1½ Starch

Olé Cheese Twists

If you're planning a cocktail party, you can make several batches of these and keep them refrigerated until you're ready to bake and serve them! They're wonderfully flavorful and finger-licking good.

🟡 Serves 8 (2 each)

> 1 cup Bisquick Reduced Fat Baking Mix
> ¼ cup cold water
> 1 teaspoon chili seasoning
> ¼ cup Kraft Fat Free Catalina Dressing
> ⅓ cup (1½ ounces) shredded Kraft reduced-fat Cheddar cheese

Preheat oven to 450 degrees. Spray a large baking sheet with butter-flavored cooking spray. In a large bowl, combine baking mix and water. Mix gently until mixture forms a soft dough. Spray a large piece of aluminum foil with butter-flavored cooking spray. On the foil, roll dough into a 10-by-12-inch rectangle. In a small bowl, combine chili seasoning and Catalina dressing. Spread dressing mixture evenly over rectangle. Evenly sprinkle Cheddar cheese over top. Fold dough lengthwise in half and pinch edges to seal. Cut into 16 (¾-inch) strips. Gently twist each strip and place twists on prepared baking sheet. Bake for 6 to 8 minutes. Serve at once.

Each serving equals:

HE: ⅔ Bread • ¼ Protein • 13 Optional Calories

74 Calories • 2 gm Fat • 2 gm Protein •
12 gm Carbohydrate • 304 mg Sodium •
47 mg Calcium • 0 gm Fiber

DIABETIC: 1 Starch

French Focaccia Luncheon Biscuits

Instead of taking the classic Italian approach to this festive open-faced bread dish, I've stirred up a tangy topping that is delightfully fresh and truly appetizing. The French would call this *délicieux!*

● Serves 6

> 1 (7.5-ounce) can Pillsbury refrigerated buttermilk biscuits
> ¼ cup (¾ ounce) grated Kraft fat-free Parmesan cheese
> 2 teaspoons dried parsley flakes
> ½ cup Kraft Fat Free French Dressing
> ¾ cup finely chopped fresh tomatoes
> ¼ cup finely chopped onion
> ⅓ cup (1½ ounces) shredded Kraft reduced-fat Cheddar cheese

Preheat oven to 400 degrees. Spray a deep-dish 10-inch pie plate with butter-flavored cooking spray. Separate biscuits and cut each into 4 pieces. In a medium bowl, combine Parmesan cheese and parsley flakes. Dip biscuit pieces first in French dressing, then in Parmesan cheese mixture. Arrange biscuit pieces in prepared pie plate. Evenly drizzle any remaining French dressing and Parmesan cheese mixture over top. Arrange tomatoes and onion over biscuit pieces. Sprinkle Cheddar cheese evenly over top. Bake for 10 to 15 minutes or until biscuits are golden brown and cheese melts. Cut into 6 wedges.

Each serving equals:

> HE: 1¼ Bread • ½ Protein • ⅓ Vegetable •
> ¼ Slider • 13 Optional Calories
> _____
> 154 Calories • 2 gm Fat • 5 gm Protein •
> 29 gm Carbohydrate • 619 mg Sodium •
> 51 mg Calcium • 3 gm Fiber
> _____
> DIABETIC: 1½ Starch/Carbohydrate • ½ Meat

Making Healthy Exchanges Work for You

You're now ready to begin a wonderful journey to better health. In the preceding pages, you've discovered the remarkable variety of good food available to you when you begin eating the Healthy Exchanges way. You've stocked your pantry and learned many of my food preparation "secrets" that will point you on the way to delicious success.

But before I let you go, I'd like to share a few tips that I've learned while traveling toward healthier eating habits. It took me a long time to learn how to eat *smarter*. In fact, I'm still working on it. But I am getting better. For years, I could *inhale* a five-course meal in five minutes flat—and still make room for a second helping of dessert!

Now I follow certain signposts on the road that help me stay on the right path. I hope these ideas will help point you in the right direction as well.

1. **Eat slowly** so your brain has time to catch up with your tummy. Cut and chew each bite slowly. Try putting your fork down between bites. Stop eating as soon as you feel full. Crumple your napkin and throw it on top of your plate so you don't continue to eat when you are no longer hungry.

2. **Smaller plates** may help you feel more satisfied by your food portions *and* limit the amount you can put on the plate.

3. **Watch portion size.** If you are *truly* hungry, you can always add more food to your plate once you've finished your initial serving. But remember to count the additional food accordingly.

4. **Always eat at your dining-room or kitchen table.** You deserve better than nibbling from an open refrigerator or over the sink. Make an attractive place setting, even if you're eating alone. Feed your eyes as well as your stomach. By always eating at a table, you will become much more aware of your true food intake. For some reason, many of us conveniently "forget" the food we swallow while standing over the stove or munching in the car or on the run.

5. **Avoid doing anything else while you are eating.** If you read the paper or watch television while you eat, it's easy to consume too much food without realizing it, because you are concentrating on something else besides what you're eating. Then, when you look down at your plate and see that it's empty, you wonder where all the food went and why you still feel hungry.

Day by day, as you travel the path to good health, it will become easier to make the right choices, to eat *smarter*. But don't ever fool yourself into thinking that you'll be able to put your eating habits on cruise control and forget about them. Making a commitment to eat good healthy food and sticking to it takes some effort. But with all the good-tasting recipes in this Healthy Exchanges cookbook, just think how well you're going to eat—and enjoy it—from now on!

Healthy Lean *Bon Appétit!*

Index of Recipes

I want to hear from you . . .

Besides my family, the love of my life is creating "common folk" healthy recipes and solving everyday cooking questions in *The Healthy Exchanges Way*. Everyone who uses my recipes is considered part of the Healthy Exchanges Family, so please write to me if you have any questions, comments, or suggestions. I will do my best to answer. With your support, I'll continue to stir up even more recipes and cooking tips for the Family in the years to come.

Write to: JoAnna M. Lund
c/o Healthy Exchanges, Inc.
P.O. Box 124
DeWitt, IA 52742

If you prefer, you can fax me at 1-319-659-2126 or contact me via e-mail by writing to HealthyJo@aol.com. Or visit my Healthy Exchanges Internet web site at http://www.healthyexchanges.com.

Now That You've Seen
Fresh from the Hearth,
Why Not Order
The Healthy Exchanges Food Newsletter?

If you enjoyed the recipes in this cookbook and would like to cook up even more of these "common folk" healthy dishes, you may want to subscribe to *The Healthy Exchanges Food Newsletter*.

This monthly 12-page newsletter contains 30-plus new recipes *every month* in such columns as:

- Reader Exchange
- Reader Requests
- Recipe Makeover
- Micro Corner
- Dinner for Two

- Crock Pot Luck
- Meatless Main Dishes
- Rise & Shine
- Our Small World

- Brown Bagging It
- Snack Attack
- Side Dishes
- Main Dishes
- Desserts

In addition to all the recipes, other regular features include:

- The Editor's Motivational Corner
- Dining Out Question & Answer
- Cooking Question & Answer
- New Product Alert
- Success Profiles of Winners in the Losing Game
- Exercise Advice from a Cardiac Rehab Specialist
- Nutrition Advice from a Registered Dietitian
- Positive Thought for the Month

Just as in this cookbook, all *Healthy Exchanges Food Newsletter* recipes are calculated in three distinct ways: 1) Weight Loss Choices, 2) Calories with Fat and Fiber Grams, and 3) Diabetic Exchanges.

The cost for a one-year (12-issue) subscription with a special Healthy Exchanges 3-ring binder to store the newsletters in is $28.50, or $22.50 without the binder. To order, simply complete the form and mail to us *or* call our toll-free number and pay with your VISA or MasterCard.

———— Yes, I want to subscribe to *The Healthy Exchanges Food Newsletter.* $28.50 Yearly Subscription Cost with Storage Binder $————

$22.50 Yearly Subscription Cost without Binder . . . . $————

———— Foreign orders please add $6.00 for money exchange and extra postage. . . . . $————

———— I'm not sure, so please send me a sample copy at $2.50 . . . . $————

Please make check payable to HEALTHY EXCHANGES or pay by VISA/MasterCard

CARD NUMBER: _____ EXPIRATION DATE: _____

SIGNATURE: _____

Signature required for all credit card orders.

Or Order Toll-Free, using your credit card, at 1-800-766-8961

NAME: _____

ADDRESS: _____

CITY: _____ STATE: _____ ZIP: _____

TELEPHONE:(____) _____

If additional orders for the newsletter are to be sent to an address other than the one listed above, please use a separate sheet and attach to this form.

MAIL TO: **HEALTHY EXCHANGES**
P.O. BOX 124
DeWitt, IA 52742-0124

1-800-766-8961 for customer orders
1-319-659-8234 for customer service

Thank you for your order, and for choosing to become a part of the Healthy Exchanges Family!

About the Author

JoAnna M. Lund, a graduate of the University of Western Illinois, worked as a commercial insurance underwriter for eighteen years before starting her own business, Healthy Exchanges, Inc., which publishes cookbooks, a monthly newsletter, motivational booklets, and inspirational audiotapes. Her first book, *Healthy Exchanges Cookbook*, has more than 500,000 copies in print. A popular speaker with hospitals, support groups for heart patients and diabetics, and service and volunteer organizations, she appears regularly on QVC, and on regional television and radio shows, and has been featured in newspapers and magazines across the country.

The recipient of numerous business awards, JoAnna was an Iowa delegate to the national White House Conference on Small Business. She is a member of the International Association of Culinary Professionals, the Society for Nutrition Education, and other professional publishing and marketing associations. She lives with her husband, Clifford, in DeWitt, Iowa.

Healthy Exchanges recipes are a great way to begin—
but if your goal is living healthy for a lifetime,

You need HELP!

JoAnna M. Lund's
Healthy Exchanges Lifetime Plan

"I lost 130 pounds and reclaimed my health following a Four Part
Plan that emphasizes not only Healthy Eating, but also Moderate
Exercize Lifestyle Changes and Goal-setting, and most important of
all, Positive Attitude."

- If you've lost weight before but failed to keep it off . . .
- If you've got diabetes, high blood pressure, high cholesterol, or
  heart disease—and you need to reinvent your lifestyle . . .
- If you want to raise a healthy family and encourage good lifelong
  habits in your kids . . .

HELP is on the way!

- The Support You Need • The Motivation You Want •
  A Program That Works•

HELP: Healthy Exchanges Lifetime Plan is available
at your favorite bookstore.